I084093З

LIBERAL CHAOS & ROT

Karen Kellock Ph.D.

Manual for Superior Men

This is a complete theory based on Einstein physics, Political Psychology, Systems Theory and Archetypal Psychiatry.

FORMULA

All success attraction
All disease obstruction
All recovery elimination

You must fast on all three

OBSTRUCTIONS:

People
Habit
Food

LIBERAL CHAOS AND ROT

It's a funny thing but those that are full of themselves are actually empty, it's compensatory see.   Sin puts us in a dark place. Sudden jealous triangles and enemies seeking to destroy the ace.   Some were complicitous--going along to get along--and some were bystanders who didn't oppose at all.   The sisters spread rumors and ruin the reputation of their sibling, spilling the beans to anybody.   This is not what's wrong with you, it's about what happened to you from liberal abuse.

TIES THAT BIND

LASTING EFFECT OF HURT
PEOPLE ARE CRUEL
MUSIC/PETS THE HIGHEST THERAPIES
MEMORIES OF YOUR PAST
NEW DOORS OPEN WITH CREEPS GONE
MODERN CHURCH HELL
STAY ALIGNED WITH GOD'S SPIRIT OR FAIL
OVERCOMING ACERBITY/RIDICULE
DECAY: TEEN MOBS/WICKED WITCHES
SICK SOULS PURSUE CONFUSION
ANOSOGNOSIC HELL
DIVINE HEDGE OF GOD'S PROTECTION
SIMPLY ACT RIGHT
INSIDIOUS SOUL TIES
OUTSIDE RELATIONSHIPS
WOMEN HAVE FLYING MONKEYS/HIT MEN
PSYCHOLOGICAL LOCKS
MARRIED RECLUSES
HERETICAL MODERN PREACHERS
HEALING ONLY WITH DISTANCE
DEVIL DIGS BITTERNESS
SEE REJECTION AS PROTECTION

TIES THAT BIND

PURSUE HIM, LOSE SELF
TOXIC MEMORIES: ADRENALIN
THE TIE YOU CAN'T ESCAPE
DENOUNCE AND BREAK THE TIE
LIFE-THREATENING TIES
FREE OF SOUL TIES/OLD NETWORKS
WORSHIPPING REJECTORS
WHY DO WOMEN WANT EM?
FLATTER WORKS WITH QUEENS CURSED
LOW SELF-WORTH ATTRACTIONS
THE APPROVAL TRAP
ADDICTED TO CHAOS
MAGNET TO MAGGOTS
MAN-WORSHIPPING
TRAUMA FROM A PRIOR GUY
SLEAZE BAGS WRAPPED NICE
TRAPPED IN FAIL GROOVES
SHORTBREAD FASTING
TACO AND NONE: REFLECTIONS
IT *ALL* CAN HAPPEN AGAIN
RUMINATIONS ON CREATIVE TRIGGERS

LIBERAL CHAOS & ROT

IF WE COULD SEE WHO WE ARE
STOP COMPLAINING AFTER BLESSING
DISTRACT FROM NEWS
KEEP THINGS IN FAMILY/STOP BLABBING
SO YOU MADE A FOOL OF YOURSELF
SAD SISTER STORIES
WHEN RIVALRY BECOMES ABUSE
EXTREME JEALOUSY IS COMMON
SISTER ABUSE AND PANIC ATTACKS
JEALOUS CHRISTIAN SIBLINGS
SIGNS OF TOXICITY IN CHRISTIAN SIBLINGS
CRITICISM IS NOT RACISM
ME AGAINST THE VISCIOUS MOB
WIN A MAN'S PROTECTION
MARITAL FIGHTING IS UGLY/PRESUMPTUOUS
THE CULPRITS PLAY VICTIM
AMERICA BEGAN AS PURITANS
THE MODERN CHURCH IS ANTI-CALVINIST
LET EM ALL IN: LIBS WANT OPEN BORDERS
THE LEFT LOVES RADICAL ISLAM
SCIENCE FICTION WOULD MAKE MORE SENSE
A LIBERAL TOWN IS HORRIBLE
GIVE UP HALF-TRUTH FOX: FOUND TIME!
SOAPS PORTRAY MORALISTS AS PSYCHOTIC
THEIR SIN WILL BE SHOUTED FROM THE ROOFTOPS
TV: WIMPS PORTRAYED AS DUMB INGRATES
WHEN YOUR WORLD HATES YOUR GUTS

LIBERAL CHAOS & ROT

INFIDELITY OVERLOAD & FEMINIST TOADS
SICK IN THE GUT—GONE TOO FAR
WE NEED STRONG LEADERS
WICKED MEN HYPNOTIZING WEAK WOMEN
MUST MANAGE PEOPLE AND BULLIES
AVOID WEAK PEOPLE & LIMP HANDSHAKES
DEMONS FROM PREVIOUS MARRIAGES
UNATTRACTIVE WOMEN: SEARED CONSCIENCES
ISOLATION IS THE BEST PROTECTION
NO LIBERTY IN THE CRAZY CITIES
LOUSY LASCIVIOUS LIBERALS
NARRATIVE CONTROLLED BY LEFT
WE MOVED TO A SAFER STATE, A FLY-OVER GREAT
FEMINISTS LOVE HILLARY, GUILTY AS HELL
STUDENTS FIT ONLY BY MOUTHING THE VISION
THEY POOH-POOHED EVERYTHING I WANTED TO DO
LUNATIC LEFT HAS MONEY, POPULARITY AND INFLUENCE
LIBERAL LOGIC WORSE THAN CORRUPTION
THE WHOLE SYSTEM HATES ONE: TRIBALISM
ANOMOLIES IN A SEPARATE REALITY/BLACK SHEEP
REJECT JUNKARDS, SLOBS AND MESSERS (PORN ADDICTS)
HILLARY AND THE HIPPIES FROM THE SIXTIES
THEY TRIED TO WRECK THE COUNTRY
PATRIOTS HATE DISORDER: CLOSE THE BORDER!
PC IS MIND CONTROL TO CREATE DIVISION
100 MILLION KILLED AND THEY WANT SANDERS/CORTEZ?
FRUGI-FATARIAN-FASTARIANISM
HOLY FAUCET, ENDLESS SPRING

TIES THAT BIND

The Cause of Mental Illness: Other People

You never have to feel this way again. The fact you're feeling it means you had to learn the lesson.

Something like a Hitler can happen again cuz people are people: if dumbed they're easily taken in.

Why are the best fighting armies the best lookin'? Because in both it requires self-discipline.

LASTING EFFECT OF HURT

Pray to forget and forgive the past while retrieving the lessons learned from losers and pests.

In this era political attitude becomes a criterion of friends and mates and baby that's ok.

Just ordinary people will hurt you more than you can ever know or predict even if the Elect.

Don't fear the future cuz the past was bleak. You're a good girl now, purity as God speaks.

It's number one: Free speech is the main thing you need to be human and survive as a nation.

If you can't marry her at least manager her career and you can make millions a year together.

Stop blaming them when it's your own dam fault hanging out with em. Affinity is nonrandom.

He snatched me out of a prickly/complicated social situation to solitude in a whole new land.

TIES THAT BIND

Extreme persecution seems to be a major stage in the Hero's Journey as it surely was with me.

An unboundaried, broken female needing approval: what a magnet to maggots and upheaval.

Eventual victory is assured and then you'll be protected from all you experienced in earlier years.

PEOPLE ARE CRUEL

People are cruel when they see ya again as if time passing is a mystery of the aging human.

He pays the bills, he keeps people away--what else would you ever need for a great day?

Having no self-awareness they can't see how they bring themselves down, their wargames well known.

Female narcissism can't be hidden and they'll stop watching you girl so stay humble woman.

Three tacos and I'm good for 48 hours and this saves me so much time and gives me power.

I don't write, I wait. For that fascinating two liner solving contradictions & tying loose ends ok.

I don't write, I wait: for that cute phrase that maybe only I understand because it's so deep ok.

Mate-selection is nonrandom. It's not so much about them but why the hell you are with em.

It's like a big club and you ain't in it. That's the feeling I got through life but now I've transcended it.

It wasn't those bad actors but Satan rising up in em because you the target were a weak woman.

TIES THAT BIND

Forget the bad actors they were just Satan's minions but painfully your MOST IMPORTANT lessons.

Stop thinking of bad actors and transcend to a higher spiritual world of artsy/creative triggers.

Bad actors or principalities and powers? See it as Satan for people aren't that important ever.

To be a good doctor be like a veterinarian: what does the patient LOOK like not numbers, aye.

MUSIC/PETS THE HIGHEST THERAPIES

Music keeps me sane in an insane world. It brings order outa chaos so I'm open as dreams unfurl.

In music I'm mentally transported to another world where I can BE anything I wanna BE.

Music organizes experience, it messages the brain and makes me happy: instantly it's all gains.

Memory detox is like an onion, unpeeling to the core. I'm now at sixteen saying "Oh My Lord!"

I take nothing for granted, what goes up can crash down: I had too many surprises long ago.

Your new diet: It worked at first and I hope it'll work again but right now it's not workin' man.

I too was a raving maniac, a female demon. A sense of entitlement rooted in narcissism & sinnin'.

MEMORIES OF YOUR PAST

It's a much bigger deal in your eyes than it is in theirs, they're too busy focused on whatever.

TIES THAT BIND

No matter how bad you were thru symbols they always saw the genius of the situation/so clever.

Little pin pricks of evil put-downs and pure maliciousness is what we get from feminists.

If I love you enough to marry you, you should have my total loyalty too like when they ridicule.

Their bitter words, their hateful voices. Like pit vipers they inject poison repeatedly in vices.

NEW DOORS OPEN WITH CREEPS GONE

New doors open with every creep you let go of friend--they hold you down/you don't need em.

Words are darts: they are a literal physical assault and I pity the poor kids of such neurotic adults.

They're like pit vipers: injecting their black poison venom spray then slithering away.

Talking to them is a physical assault as their words as darts tear thru your defenses: build em up.

To call it acerbity is such an understatement to me. These are wicked witches from Satan see.

Since you can't predict what's gonna come outa their stupid mouths all you can do is stay alone.

It was ridicule all the way up the ladder but now my reward is a locked gate/all that matters.

We swim in muddy waters. We get alot on us, we don't know any better but then we see it all later.

MODERN CHURCH HELL

TIES THAT BIND

Personally, I hate religion: I just love God and His word which inoculates us from evil in the world.

Religion--the traditions of men--are a bunch of glass concepts that shatter/are so boring man.

Just get to know God and forget the traditions of men and boring meetings with fake friends.

The world of God exposes anything toxic to the soul so just read those--now you're outa the cold.

Sin and repentance, heaven or hell: that's all I wanna hear about but these meetings are a dull pill.

The modern church makes up stuff shown in little "skits" but it's not from God just twits.

The modern church has its own hymns and avoids those of old which talk of hell, heaven and sin.

STAY ALIGNED WITH GOD'S SPIRIT OR FAIL

When the soul--mind/will/emotions--gets disconnected from the spirit of God we then worship men.

Soul ties develop and the backdrop is sex: the most basic primal urge takes over, a definite hex.

The soul is directed by the SPIRIT of God but when it's not it gets embroiled in toxic human knots.

Just worship God your Father and you're impervious to soul ties about which you're in a lather.

Anything in us which is out of alignment with the spirit is exposed in the word of God so read it all.

People fear anything different so on the way up the ladder ridicule rules and it's a bummer.

TIES THAT BIND

Soul ties are not real love but oh, how they feel like it dove! See the difference and then live.

The value of freedom is not known until it's lost: being tyrannized by anything has a high cost.

Government should just be a watch guard not a giant leviathan controlling speech and everythin'.

OVERCOMING ACERBITY/RIDICULE

If married to a drunkard principalities and powers take over and the spouse is shoved down under.

To be a giant success you must overcome the biggest stress: the acerbity of envy in your pests.

Your emotions as deep as the oceans should be transmuted to beneficial creative action.

All I know is: God is my father in heaven. To see a good example of Dad watch the Rifleman.

Americana is best displayed in the Old West: attitude of self-defense for ONE goal--independence.

"Home is all" to me as it should be to every woman. That's why we're happiest there: heaven.

Feminists separated us from our home and made homemaking inferior--they ridiculed us all.

Just do your work then wait to be discovered. You planted a helluva seed/wait like a farmer.

No more news and interviews, now it's just home, dogs, cats and enjoying breathtaking views.

Religion: boring meetings, petty hierarchies & socializing but to man's traditions God says NO see.

TIES THAT BIND

Aspirants: You know you'll eventually make it so just be patient and continue self-improvement.

Don't compete with spouse. If she's so much better at such you do the business and make $$MUCH.

Don't outa pity go down a rabbit hole with them. They'll clobber you dead, it's not worth it friend.

Clever immigrants making it with weak and traumatized white women who will even pay them.

God judged you on how you're gonna be & that's how he dealt with your enemies/even then see.

Floridians are like little ants, building everything back up immediately and making it all pretty.

DECAY: TEEN MOBS/WICKED WITCHES

Teen mobs attacking lone nerds who object to dirty words: We're now ruled by evil children sir.

Men: stand against wicked witches whether they be mother, lover, sister, neighbor, office worker.

Wicked witches kill children in the womb and it means dismemberment: amputation's assumed.

They are wicked witches by a priori reasoning: they vote dem which wants abortion up to birth see.

True leaders defend the weak. Men: stand against evil witches who kill the weakest: SPEAK!

Black women rule now. They are everywhere on TV talkin' shit on ALL the white people, wow.

If you can't speak the truth you gotta put it in nursery rhymes or other innocent disguises, aye.

TIES THAT BIND

This administration failed because it was concerned with optics rather than actual reality.

I too let a snake into my house who needed help who then struck and quickly used me up.

Their entire matrix is coddling criminals and allowing victims to suffer. That's dems/bummers.

We swim in muddy waters and literally don't know any better but with repentance it gets clearer.

Similar to Nazi Germany, MOST of the pop are hypnotized/you can't reason with em see.

Sweep it out: thats power of the word of God. Otherwise the world suffocates/we're flawed.

Signs the soul is broken, disconnected from spirit of God: when deciding to move away that's all.

SICK SOULS PURSUE CONFUSION

The soul is sick pursuing one who disagrees, consumed with that one who's spiritually contradicting.

Their words constantly disturb your peace but you want em day and night: it's a broken soul, aye.

Because soul ties are addictive systems they are sick, as you return to the harm that person inflicts.

They don't agree with your spirit, yet you're consumed with them? This was the past/it's over, amen.

By intentionally moving from the will of God, cuz you love that clod, shows this broken bond.

Constantly--CONSTANTLY--thinking/wanting the one who contradicts is how the devil works.

TIES THAT BIND

Out of the will of God your spirit is grieved and your soul consumed so then you worship man too.

Consumed, you allow things to happen that shouldn't, making excuses which before you wouldn't.

He puts his hands on you, humiliates you publicly or cheats visibly: yours is a broken spirit lady.

It's the wife of the alcoholic who is called a "drunken alcoholic" as she drinks for solace.

ANOSOGNOSIC HELL

Just cuz the alki's lost pattern recognition [anosognosia] doesn't mean he can't manipulate situations.

Anosognosia means he's impaired from seeing his own condition: a blank spot in his perception.

Killing yourself but unable to see you are killing yourself: that's the addict's anosognosic hell.

Ageism: unnecessary hurt. Yes I've spent more years on earth but that makes me better not worse.

You're have a massive soul tie and don't know what to do about it. Then later it's hard to forget it.

I'm so glad to be out of a southern California liberal desert town. I wrote 100 books on the clowns.

They all voted for Obama and gay orgies were everywhere. Small houses with constant cars.

Liberals aren't for freedom, they're accusatory and dumbed down. It's persecution full-blown.

They way the women looked at me with hate in their eyes. They had no reason, I was despised.

TIES THAT BIND

DIVINE HEDGE OF GOD'S PROTECTION

The men were lecherous and kept coming to my house. I had to fight em off and I had **NO** solace.

In my immaturity I drank to deal with the situation and then the whole dam evil world flowed in.

When the divine hedge of God is down, wow: you're on streets unprotected, in the cold now.

I messed up for the last shameless time, the hedge was down: in came the users/abusers/gutter slime.

I've been wrong in life and learned the only solution was returning to factory settings thru fasting.

Before I had a locked gate I couldn't plan any day, it was left to fate but now I'm in control ok?

SIMPLY ACT RIGHT

Simply act right and all will change, you'll bring respect. It's as simple as that for the lay or Elect.

Why didn't you act right? Weakness allowed autonomisms bursting out, starting fights.

Be strong, act right and love the Lord as **ALL** returns to normal, a hedge of protection around y'all.

She's not happy he has two other women, she has lost herself that's all—to the power of demons.

When someone's controlling your mind your only hope is to get back to God. Now clarity/no clouds.

Discouragement/disappointment is not "depression" so don't give me that, things always upturn man.

TIES THAT BIND

Studies show 70% of women flake on you. This is relieving since it's happened so often/whew.

Women bring their own house down with their own two hands because they listened to girlfriends.

Get back to God to destroy this stronghold over your life. Addiction to people is pure strife.

Women all over world see anti-depressants as "happy pills". Bloats your face/thoughts are nil.

Our founders gave two reasons for guns: tyrannical governments and roaming lunatic mobs.____

INSIDIOUS SOUL TIES

The soul is sick when one gets what he desired but he's always miserable after ditching the good.

A sick soul constantly pursues happiness but never finds it. It's here now but he rejects that.

Greener pastures: They believe the new relationship will work but it won't cuz the soul is sick sir.

She left a nice man who supported her for a jerk who used her. He left a sweet lady for a chaser.

Never being satisfied--the restless spirit--always hates what it has and wants what it doesn't, aye.

A soul tie makes us crush people who've been loyal, the very foundation of our success, foiled.

Outa the will of God, listening to some joker, she leaves a great man for a fool who doesn't love her.

Lured on the internet her flesh shakes on her bones and she leaves her family and lovely home.

TIES THAT BIND

Some woman games him, calling him "Hercules" and instantly he wants her and starts to sneak.

A sick soul disarranged from God is susceptible as greener pastures consumes/becomes all.

Insidious soul ties will make one abuse those who've been nothing but loyal: what a way to go.

Soul ties make the victim so confused she turns on the most loyal and any other supporters too.

My friend in whom I trusted lifted up his heel against me--a soul tie cued him to misperceive.

A soul ties is a trash relationship: garbage. And now she wants to cash in her history for this?

OUTSIDE RELATIONSHIPS

He got her into his car at lunchtime, telling her how fine she was. A soul tie formed, she left her hus.

If you have home problems, take care of it. Don't go out on a side situation, be better than that.

If he "ain't no good" it's no excuse for side dish. Do the legal things, recover, then make a switch.

In the will of God you have a comfy home and a nice husband who maintains your throne.

Degrading and disrespecting yourself on the streets is not who you are, whether online or caller.

A soul tie makes you think you love this guy but it's all based on sex, the deepest primal high.

Her self-estimation increasingly drops as she does worse and worse, invaded by users/frauds.

TIES THAT BIND

Aligned with God, it was due to her husband she had all that but now she's a homeless doormat.

Women, learn this lesson. Don't leave your nice husband for greener pastures or you're done.

Tellin' you something about your mother: She may be of the feather that gossips about her daughter.

Helluva thing to remember her by but she caused you infinite trouble all through your life.

WOMEN HAVE FLYING MONKEYS/HIT MEN

Her daughters/sons followed her, they were her flying monkeys and you were the target honey.

They're thick as bricks in with this witch but nobody's on your side, that would mean ditched.

Mom hated your boyfriend but when he called she used him as a trash bin for all her gossipin'

It hurts like hell to face these family evils. The Greek tragedies were all about family ya' know.

Sting shots and poison word darts, that's what I got from her. She's the authority, it's war.

A narcissist idolizes then minimizes then discards or claims credit for everything which is worse.

Be a teacher to teachers and preachers but not to the rabble, you're too sensitive/they'll kill you.

Repent then it never happened. Buried in the deepest ocean and God put a sign: Don't Go Fishin'.

There was an EVENT that changed the way you view the world and the way that you view yourself.

TIES THAT BIND

The life-changing **EVENT**: The issue is: can you exit the event or be permanently trapped in it?

Forgiveness is the process of moving out of an event rather than allowing it to hold you down.

After the toxic event we either forgive to walk out of it or it becomes a life-long story, trapped by it.

PSYCHOLOGICAL LOCKS

This storyline after an event becomes a psychological lock and for any mental evolution, that's it.

We can be so psychologically locked we don't recognize liberation when it comes/blocked out.

Rejection is one of life's great challenges. When people don't want you, distance yourself fast.

The utter turmoil when you refuse to let go of people who long ago let go of you is awful.

When his men turned against David retreated into his own personal space. Never force it/face it.

Never force yourself on them/NEVER beg like a weak and stupid woman. Retreat: heaven.

Forcing yourself on people disgraces your heavenly Father and dishonors you His son/daughter.

Never force yourself into spaces where you're not clearly wanted. I shudder to think about it.

Never go where you're tolerated, only where you're celebrated and you'll eventually make it.

David was psychologically healthy enough to separate himself from the crowd, content with God.

TIES THAT BIND

It is a miserable existence being addicted to the social since people will let you down ya' know.

When backstabbed you're strong enough in your own identity to backtrack into your sanctuary.

Be so solid with God when you separate from people there is NO sensed loss of identity at all.

For your value and worth you and God are ENOUGH. Get that settled: people/social = fluff.

There are people in your home or car who don't really want you it's just the using human zoo.

If they won't receive nor hear you, when you depart dust off your hands and say: goodbye fools!

If they receive you leave a blessing. If they don't leave them where they are and start dusting.

As a son/daughter of God you're never in the begging position. If they don't want you leave em.

MARRIED RECLUSES

He went to Vietnam, he saw headless bodies. Now that he's an elder he just wants solitude see.

They just wanna be alone even if married. I understand this perfectly cuz I'm the same way see.

Why is DISTANCE so important? HEALING can't begin until then = hate is always hurtful.

As long as you stay with haters/rejectors healing can never take place while it's you they break.

After going through all those painful and embarrassing lessons it's like God just erased em.

TIES THAT BIND

Not only did he erase all my mistakes He bulldozed down the desert cabin I made em in ok.

God is so good He doesn't want his sons/daughters to be weighed down with the past/remorse.

Besides they're all dead or gone anyway, or didn't see the relevance of what happened for today.

HERETICAL MODERN PREACHERS

Nothing embarrasses me more than heretical modern preachers stomping the stage: bores!

Modern heretical preachers won't talk of hell and heaven, sin and repentance--hell no!

That's what makes them heretical--do they ever condemn abortion or homosexual?

They don't wanna offend laity cuz who'd come to the sanctuary and most importantly, give money?

A good preacher finds ways to raise money other than lying to the laity about sin/repentance see.

Joel Osteen: they all copy him by not stepping on toes and saying everything's all right/no remorse.

Sin will keep you longer than planned, keep you trapped/flat and cost you WAY more man.

Forgiveness is the only way to get outa psychological jail when the perpetrators don't care at all.

Ok so he can dance, but is he into repentance? Cuz that's the measure of man thru centuries.

HEALING ONLY WITH DISTANCE

TIES THAT BIND

You will never heal from these insidious mental stab wounds until you disengage/move on.

Despite words of love when actions indicate they don't want you DISTANCE is needed now Sue.

If they want you you can feel it. If they wanna use you you feel psychologically degraded.

David didn't take revenge or plot his return, he just sought distance. DISTANCE is all girl.

Secondly, reach for a spiritual perspective. Rejection hurts but not when you pray and transcend it.

Rejection: the last thing to do is fall on your face, and in front of inferior men? It's a disgrace.

With rejection most people fall into the flesh. It never works, it does not serve, it's a downward turn.

DEVIL DIGS BITTERNESS

The devil wants to establish a root in bitterness, for you to be offended, it becomes a stronghold.

When rejected by PEOPLE you must get in the face of God to get HIS perspective on evil.

The spiritual's the only way leading you to peace, life, God and righteousness. Take it sis.

You must take a spiritual view cuz you can't make sense of rejection, not when your heart's right too.

Your heart is broken cuz you did your part and they've not reciprocated. But God weighs it.

This person does not want you and you can't process it. You must SHIFT cuz God has allowed it.

TIES THAT BIND

You can't get a revelation of WHY God's allowed it: by walking in the flesh you will never know it.

In the spirit you see the life of God in it but in the flesh it only means death: like you drinking at it.

The rejection of people is usually a sign that God has accepted you. He wants way more for you.

SEE REJECTION AS PROTECTION

The rejection of man is the protection of God, recall that when your heart breaks by the flawed.

Rejection has little to do with you but your heavenly father: "rejoice when men reject you".

Seek God's heart/thoughts on this matter and you'll feel so much better as His daughter.

Thirdly, make your plans to win. Don't mislabel the rejection of people as a sign of failure friend.

Rejection is such a sting people spiral downwards. But what if a blessing from God? Look forward.

You don't need them to win, God and you is enough to pull this off. Don't mislabel or get hung up.

God has a plan for you to come outa this on TOP. Pursue this plan, about this guy don't talk.

And David said "should I pursue?" and God said "yes--and get back everything they took too".

Thanks to God who ALWAYS causes us to triumph. We're winners when free of the dross.

In the presence of God you make your plans to WIN since that is always/irrevocably His plan.

TIES THAT BIND

Finally, hold nothing against them. You wanna be a clear channel for God to work thru friend.

Allowing bitterness to take root makes you just like them. Forgiveness is getting outa prison.

Take distance, see God's perspective, plan to win, hold nothing against them and now: success.

A soul tie is a mental connection that ties us to a person whom God has not ordained for our lives.

It's a stronghold war: Leaders form ungodly soul ties with followers and become controllers.

PURSUE HIM, LOSE SELF

Her pursuit of a man causes her to lose herself: the wrong path chosen on how she FELT.

Losing yourself in the pursuit of someone else makes you not recognize the loss of magic/hell.

She knows it's unhealthy and ungodly but she can't break free. It's a massive soul tie see.

The soul--mind, will and emotions--is tied up in a knot and you can't stop THINKING of them.

She can will herself to break free but somehow her will adjusts and she keeps running back see.

A relationship that's not ordained of God and does not serve you well: that's a soul tie from hell.

We're not to be unequally yoked with unbelievers, for what do you really have in common girl?

He's ungodly, very worldly, coarse and seems to disdain all she values yet she's tied thru and thru.

TIES THAT BIND

Soul ties can be sexual but also hooked to an early trauma where he becomes like momma.

A soul tie is a dysfunctional or not really helpful relationship and it's nothing but hardship.

She's unequally [weirdly] yoked to some jerk and that's the end of trust, promotion and the perks.

TOXIC MEMORIES: ADRENALIN

Toxic memories: To obliterate those neural pathways, when they come don't give em any energy.

Toxic memories flooding with adrenalin: don't let this happen cuz it makes the groove deepen.

When she came against me I was terrified of the misjudgment, the archetype evoked see.

To be misjudged and spoken to like that, I never wanted to see the witch again, dumbed and fat.

It's a definite soul tie when their souls don't jive but what do we know maybe it's God, aye.

Why is this queen riding with this clown? Thoughts like that prevail when a soul tie's involved.

Why is this king with her? It's an unequal yoke, a soul tie, somehow she's a mental space renter.

Soul ties are the great tragedy of casual sex which is an unseen/unwritten contract and a hex.

Don't give the memory any energy. When it pops up again nip it in the bud, knowing the theory.

Both unequal yoke and soul ties are things you shouldn't be in and feel impossible to get out: war.

TIES THAT BIND

I too got stuck, many times. Tears on my pillow for years, decades, on the begging end to slime.

The yoke is something you know you shouldn't be in but is impossible to get out of, to my chagrin.

Unequal yokes and soul ties are both things you know better against but can't escape the hex.

Sick system: Part of you wants out of the dysfunction but another part pulls you back in.

THE TIE YOU CAN'T ESCAPE

The soul tie you can't escape is unprofitable and uncomfortable/soon it's no longer a thrill.

A wife feels "unmet needs" so develops a soul tie and ear with a man in town/brings down her home.

The soul tie pulls her outa her house away from her family, following an illusion as such.

She is hypnotized by her own language as she uses it to describe this bogus relationship.

A stallion yoked to a donkey is obvious but she changes this reality through language to a positive.

Most folks trapped in soul ties are self-deceived from the language they use. Face it then move.

DENOUNCE AND BREAK THE TIE

You must denounce this bond by using language against it. Turn the thing around to be rid of it.

RESIST the devil and he will flee--use strong language against it even if you feel you love it.

TIES THAT BIND

Come out from amongst em so I can receive you: gotta separate first then success occurs too.

Use strong language to denounce it even if still stuck in it. That's a step up to no longer value it.

To break soul tie your heart must break so your soul can heal. Go thru fire tho' it hurts like hell.

You must eliminate the LIE God wants you in this. You've manufactured a fantasy delusion sis.

Bringing the soul tie to the altar: despite abuse she thinks making it legal is a marriage-maker.

Her false and toxic religion makes her think God wants her stuck in this: "keep sweet" despite the dis.

LIFE-THREATENING TIES

The soul tie even in marriage is life-threatening but the false religious insist you stay with him.

Eliminate the lie keeping you stuck: That God joins ALL things together--uh-uh, He hates this stuff.

Making covenants with people which God has nothing to do with, a yoke of the false religionists.

God's done most of the work for you, by isolating you and preventing all contact: amazing, shrewd.

Stop speaking language breathing life into a mirage. This was all your head trip/camouflaged.

Instead of obsessing over him or her, all you gotta do is take this time and open up to your Father.

Tapping into God is a journey you'll never forget. It's the SPIRIT man, blocked by a fantasy tidbit.

TIES THAT BIND

In your private time tell God "I need you". How hard is that? New vistas open up, rid of the rat.

Draw nigh to God, He'll draw nigh to you, that's His promise. Just stop, get rid of: welcome bliss.

Reach UP to God, He reaches DOWN to you. I can't express the relief you'll experience soon.

FREE OF SOUL TIES/OLD NETWORKS

They sought to kill me, surrounded by snakes and scorpions. God snatched me out/free again.

They made me so insane with false accusations I developed a Fatal Mental Disorder when young.

God's gave me double for my trouble: a nice home behind a wall and locked gate is paradisiacal.

Where finally every moment is my own and I'm NEVER adapting to other people: PARADISIACAL!

As a Christian you're supposed to come out free: bondage broken not how you started woman.

What a refreshing breeze as you repeat after me: This soul tie is finally broken outa your life see.

Along with this soul tie prepare to be free of everyone you knew. God's plans are thru the roof!

They hated you for being Christian not so much being in sin for they love that, it's just like them.

Finally, you're free--after a lifetime of the same type of repeated soul ties--and it's a cosmic party.

All the trouble a soul tie caused you is finally over, water under the bridge: it made you poor/now you're rich.

TIES THAT BIND

Picture a big balloon picking you up and taking you far far away, forever free of the fray!

Picture yourself forever free of that person, an abuser. For this is what God wants, it's true reality.

God will rescue you. It's not His will this debacle so open up to someone near you/flee like a miracle.

This is your season to break free: the Season of Treason is over for it was hell on earth see.

Be your own housekeeper lest you mal-adapt to personalities/put downs/theft of employees.

Finally free of plots and personalities, for the first time in life you can have success and prosperity.

I recall what it's like to have to adapt to people I disdained, I felt trapped and dismayed.

People are the biggest persecutors--not cats, dogs, horses or cows. Stay home/walk proud.

The greatest healthgiving luxury is solitude from people if you choose. Most can't/they're screwed.

Whatever negative emotion like fear, knowing God doesn't want it makes you snap out of it.

Why do want those who don't want us and don't want those who want us? Chasing nuts/dust.

WORSHIPPING REJECTORS

Why is it human nature to despise those who want us and worship those who don't? Huh

What is my type? One who recognizes my value that's who--not anyone who does not, whew.

TIES THAT BIND

When Samson was betrayed he lost power, status, vision, identity, purpose and his link to God.

His sick desire for her was used against him. Wanting the apathetic means you're used ab nauseam.

He ran after someone who did not want him and was stripped of his power, purpose and vision.

WHY DO WOMEN WANT EM?

Women mistake lust for love, that's why they pursue men who don't really want em/are rough.

A woman with broken consciousness believes she's wanted because she's seen as sexiness.

She's immensely attracted to this little man calling her "desirable, sexy, beautiful and lovable."

Flattery pursues her for the night not for the rest of her life but a broken queen can't see that.

FLATTER WORKS WITH QUEENS CURSED

The world makes her think her wealth is in her body. Here it starts: disorders of all types see.

Women today [who are not taught] believe all their value's in their looks: it's evil/their kooks.

Real men are attracted to your soul not body and they are not sexually aggressive as a result see.

But when the queen's soul is broken she looks for physical attractions not soul connections.

She bypasses the man who wants to get to know the real her and goes for the lecher-flatterer.

TIES THAT BIND

Women too often want men who lust for them--their bodies--caring nothing for their souls.

The broken female is drawn in by this lust over her sexy body and consents to being used, sadly.

"He makes me feel like a real woman" and here all he's doing is the same game he's always done.

He's using her body and abusing her mind but doesn't think of that: need LIFE DANGER signs.

She hated all men, not realizing her pitiful lack of boundaries drew the wrong ones in.

When caught in this matrix her self-worth is constantly dropping: drip, drip, down to the bottom.

Why attracted to uninterested men? She's attracted to what she believes she deserves, amen.

Subconscious settings of a woman's soul will never choose anything above it's self-portrait role.

LOW SELF-WORTH ATTRACTIONS

Low self-worth women attract rough necks, femme men, don't wanna work men, the noncommitted.

A woman's degree of self-worth always shows up in the quality of those allowed to occupy.

All we gotta do to get your self-portrait is to observe the person you're comfortable settling with.

Will they feel contrite they misjudged you? Don't count on it, they're also dumb/distracted too.

We pick those who abuse us over those who honor us because we don't honor ourselves.

TIES THAT BIND

We're attracted to what we think we deserve so with broken consciousness there is great danger.

The broken soul passes the good man up by calling him "boring" or "not my type" due to self-hate.

Truth: She is incapable of loving anyone who loves her soul more than she loves herself.

It's not that he's boring but that she's broken. She chooses clowns in that comfort zone.

She's caught in the "approval trap" of choosing men who reject so she may correct the past.

The men are fundamentally flawed and lack the inner fortitude to give her a real life too.

She's addicted to chaos so can't choose anything else. It's not so much attraction as it is brokenness.

Elitism telling us what to do or freedom and liberty—something not had in other countries?

THE APPROVAL TRAP

We allow, tolerate and settle for things while the broken soul passes the good man off as boring.

Thirsty for approval, she picks men who don't want her to correct the rejection from long ago

She allows/tolerates/settles for things while her broken soul passes the good man off as boring.

The issue lands on one man to finally approve of her after the other one only rejected her.

Her real desire is for the man who broke her to come back so she settles for someone like that.

TIES THAT BIND

Caught up in the Approval Trap she chooses men who don't choose her until final repentance.

The Approval Trap is why she chases men who are running from her. It's all compensatory sir.

He comes thru Friday night with an excuse to leave in an hour and it's ok you're treated as a whore.

It was her father who broke her heart so she chose men who looked like him to repair the start.

She keeps choosing the flawed who lack the fortitude to give her what she needs, being truly loved.

The Approval Trap is a psychological hold a lucky man has on her totally from her past beaus.

It stems from an early love affair when abandoned and betrayed horribly and it stuck see.

Many if not most modern women spend a life choosing these cats who never choose em back.

He'll sleep with her, spend her money and waste her time but she needs approval of this guy.

ADDICTED TO CHAOS

Addicted to chaos she wants what she can't have. Peace is problematic for a broken soul, alas.

Anything healthy can't be tolerated by a broken soul in need of adrenalin—can you even imagine?

She likes living on the edge. A safe settled man ain't attractive cuz he's too predictable [hex].

She's a woman with self-destructive appetites. Like a food addict there's no higher governing, aye.

TIES THAT BIND

Female slave conditioning is so infused she surely feeds narcissistic ego-driven male demands too.

Toxic attraction is at the heart of female slave conditioning, reinforced by Hollywood see.

Bad boys are sexy/dangerous men thrilling to know. Womanizers attract her, not the predictable.

She wants a man who no woman can tame. She's been addicted to chaos from an early age.

She can't stand a man who goes to work & comes home with no drama or need to hide his phone.

Addicted to chaos she causes trouble for the good man until he leaves her flat & now he attracts her.

I was suddenly up and then suddenly down. I know what can happen without the favor of God.

Thought I'd have a little snort and what was up came down with a splash and I failed of course.

MAGNET TO MAGGOTS

They that put light for darkness, darkness for light; bitter for sweet and sweet for bitter, aye.

Addicted to chaos she can't tell right from wrong, quality from bunk or a prince from a skunk.

You're taking a clown in a crown: "he's my king" and ignoring reliability and a stable home.

Her subconscious program is governed by appetites not discipline, another rudderless woman.

Every species has its genotype and that of man is GENIUS--in all fields, it rejuvenates us.

TIES THAT BIND

Self-preservation be damned, tho' it's not been working for a long time she serves a past demon.

MAN-WORSHIPPING

A woman chasing people and men reflects her low value of herself. Good grief woman, get a life.

What causes mental illness? Other people. How do they do it? Soul ties which are demonic/evil.

It's automatic when God's left out that we worship man and THAT'S where all the trouble starts.

Romans: Worshipping the created not the Creator: man worship's at the basis of soul ties sir.

We man-worship with lost faith/disappointment or hanging in there cuz we don't need em?

Once you witness/hold that violence in your soul you're far more careful than in youth/so bold.

Of course we all want esteem of our peers but how to get it without losing the self as a seer?

I've seen violence/how fast things can change. I'm meek/docile to God's warnings to escape.

Why does she want he who doesn't want her? She wants a man the world sees as superior.

I was trapped with buffoons and couldn't escape. I know what freedom is from my early days.

It's good to know I'm not that important cuz that keeps me humble and that means creative.

What is the power couple? These are socials who want what the world says is desirable that's all.

TIES THAT BIND

Stop thinking of old posts and how you're gonna show them. Go forward to fame/world renowned.

TRAUMA FROM A PRIOR GUY

It's been a helluva rocky ride controlled by soul ties resulting from TRAUMA with a prior guy.

The best revenge is a life well lived and now you're rockin' it, in your groove, making a mint.

You're one of the greatest geniuses that ever lived in your niche, field or peculiar occupation.

The world: a way to subsidize and empty one's self-esteem with popular impressions of success.

Odd girl in a small town is quickly seen as deviant and destroyed as a witch: stay in your niche.

If any man loveth the world the love of the Father's not in him: lust of the flesh, eyes, pride of life.

The world passeth away and lust thereof but he who does will of God abides forever [triumphs].

Time to bring good men outa closets and teach respect for them and our freedoms or forget it.________

She enters a soul tie by ignoring the voice of spirit which her flesh overrides-- now she pays the price.

The mind is bound and locked in a soul tie. The true mate is hidden behind this relational lie.

A soul mate aligns spiritually and emotionally in divine purpose to flow together in things of God.

A soul tie makes her constantly unavailable to the good man waiting in the wings and able.

TIES THAT BIND

A whoremonger thinks there's no impact from illicit sex but a mature man sees it was a giant hex.

It has such a giant impact that once God has washed his mind of it he can't even recollect it.

He must be delivered before God sends a wife cuz his mind is everywhere and filled with strife.

Soul ties develop with married people who to their own spouse become emotionally unavailable.

Jezebel stirs his flesh and pride up with "your wife doesn't know what she has" and such.

The biggest weapon the enemy uses to bind & block us from happy success is illicit relationships.

SLEAZE BAGS WRAPPED NICE

I don't care how the sleaze bag is wrapped he's still a swarmy spirit and I wouldn't trust it.

Smarmy generation/eras: smug, ingratiating, falsely earnest with low sleazy taste or quality.

No sleazy past times--God won't reward your silent crimes, you gotta be on top of things.

It's a sad thing when someone spirals down and there's nothing to stop this fallen hero free fall.

No one could stop me when I fell before inferior men and spiraled down to hell for quite a spell.

They're ideological bigots: discriminating on political world view. They end nuts/began in middle.

She had a massive soul tie with a guy which wrecked her home, career, kids and pets due to a lie.

TIES THAT BIND

It is so dangerous she must AFFIRM her intention to get out, now. Face it then say it with words gal.

A soul tie is demonic and not good for you, not what God wants and becomes vulgar/crude.

A soul tie shows how mental illness is created by other people. And when the glue is sex, wow.

A soul tie diverts attention so family & spouse are ignored: always thinking about him, lured.

TRAPPED IN FAIL GROOVES

She's so trapped in the wrong groove success is blocked and why WOULD she be rewarded by God?

This is how mental illness is created by other people and the mere contact can conquer a weak girl.

Release soul tie to get your life/destiny back cuz if you waste time on this cad your future is black.

In some women the jealousy/envy is so deep there is nothing that can stop their hate & hostility.

I write this not from what I learned in school but my "Ph.D. in the Streets"-- interacting with creeps.

If you mess with a liberal your whole life will be upside down. Don't let em in/their advice is rotten.

Finally you can do things your way without interruption so the whole day's fun: that's retirement.

Let go of dead weight/that old argument of late and you'll feel so free and light, fun and bright.

The horrible price of calumny is that everyone believes it without checking it out: no judge/no jury.

TIES THAT BIND

Dudes are dirty but women are crown of God's creation and shouldn't be operating like them.

Due to trauma and the internet women have roving eyes now. They also flake out, it's predictable.

Don't be scared of the past, thinking it'll repeat itself. That was way down the ladder in hell.

Obviously you had to experience these things to decide against them or you wouldn't have been in em.

Let things evolve on their own, never force your work. Genius knows best insights are in leisure.

WAIT until you can't help but start. WAIT for God's cue then it's automatic and without thought.

It's just a pissing contest: hix politix. Don't get involved, do your work and have success.

SHORTBREAD FASTING

God removed all hunger then fasted me for ten painless & fascinating days and I was AMAZED.

A Daily Fastarian is not an anorexic so you can shove your ED clinics run by batty food tyrants.

Shortbread: I want glucose energy in sugar/flour and from delicious butter, the satiety power.

If you wanna look your age, eat meat. If you wanna look ageless no matter what age, don't eat it.

Shortbread fasting breaks all the rules: they say NO sugar, NO flour and NO butter, fools!

Fasting consciousness is highest intelligence and that's why I shortbread fast: what a BLAST!

TIES THAT BIND

To stay on the beam we gotta fast constantly it seems or at least skillfully navigate what we eat.

Shortbread cookies in the freezer and ultra-clean kitchen or constantly fixing/cleanin?

Butter collapses calories so you don't have to eat as often and thus you get skinny as a totem.

They're down on butter and sugar the very things giving it power: satiety and energy together.

Satiety Power [SP] is more important than antioxidants cuz fasting is the highest healer/fastest.

Take your shortbread cookie and enter the world of no-hunger/fatigue fasting, it's very exciting.

I now see all that sugar and carb is for perception, perspicacity and to be all that I can be.

Perspicacity: having a ready insight into things: shrewdness. I gotta have carbs for this.

TACO AND NONE: REFLECTIONS

Three tacos and I'm good for 48 hours. These are rolling fasts, who said we have to eat every 24.

The Indians started a fast with corn, I start one with nuts. Feast then fast, get over the hump.

All wrong diets seem to work at first. It's the devil's lure but he waits and soon you're a dinosaur.

Suddenly the whole body itches as land mines dissolve into the blood and come out in the lymph.

I'd love to have a beer but dare not dear it'll start me off on a toot due to anosognosia I declare.

TIES THAT BIND

The mere atom--even cough medicine--brings it on as the whole system lights up: drink up man.

I write all day while in a proprioceptive journey from which there's no return, only while fasting.

Daily fasting is not anorexia but my-oh-my how it throws liberal women into panic in obese America.

Skin looks worse before it gets better. The stuff dislodges from cell wall, in blood to the outer.

Land of milk & honey. Milk's the butter, honey's the sugar and wheat's the flour: shortbread see?

Shortbread's not about nutrients but [SP] Satiety Power: enabled to FAST many more hours.

IT *ALL* CAN HAPPEN AGAIN

If it happened in WWII it can happen again and IS happening friends: giant downturns/trends.

Cultural Marxism deliberately bifurcates society into a victim group and the oppressor group see.

Retraditionalization: wave of the future. We're wildly sick of wokism and CNN's imploding for sure.

To liberal women "diversity" means whatever "they say" and there is no logic beyond that see.

"Barbarians" are invaders lining up on the wall of a failing society and to America, goodbye.

RUMINATIONS ON CREATIVE TRIGGERS

I did it and every word is original. That's gotta mean something, man hours times fifty after all.

TIES THAT BIND

Relocated, a locked gate, total solitude with music, views, good herb and pets is a great day.

Two liners are what I do. I was born to do it but who knew? It took a lifetime to even get a clue.

Sometimes it's more fruitful to wait than to work. This is the principal of leisure/creative triggers.

Try to wait not work, it'll always be better when you can't help but do it lured by divine spark.

Nothing more productive than looking out the window in a muse because creativity is happening too.

Tedious reading all morning or looking out the window and listening to music singing/dancing?

I don't want more input I want INNER thoughts triggered by time-honored techniques by me, boss.

LIBERAL CHAOS & ROT

IF WE COULD SEE WHO WE ARE

If we could see who we are we'd fall in awe or horror of what we've made of ourselves. C S Lewis.

You can't go on plane without that mask but if you're an illegal then come on in, mask optional.

Liberals actually think conservative speech is more offensive than Isis beheading videos see.

It's a funny thing but those that are full of themselves are actually empty, it's compensatory see.

Sin puts us in a dark place. Sudden jealous triangles and enemies seeking to destroy the ace.

You don't just sin, repent and forget it. It sets a whole chain of dark reactions then it's groupthink.

Then it's groupthink: one's shame hands over control to others and this is a spiraling down to stink.

Her sinning in reaction to his drinking gives him the control of groupthink then she's the fink.

She felt blame for others molestations. After a time of being put upon she's truly mentally lame.

She felt guilt, blame and shame all her life to the point of pathology tho' she was the victim see.

How much is inherited shame or grafted in guilt from victimhood in your life? It crippled me, aye.

You repent/change/relocate but now have PTSD from memories with gains you don't appreciate.

CHAOS & ROT PREFACE

STOP COMPLAINING AFTER BLESSING

God blessed my socks off and gave me double for my trouble and still I was past-resentful.

No matter what we did It's all erased with repentance but I couldn't believe that/was still mad at.

Sitting in your castle God blessed you with thinking of someone 30 years ago you're angry with.

God was the One who gave you/allowed you this but here you sit, angry at some past twit.

Use divine LOGIC to get outa PTSD memories. Use the cross and what you KNOW about it see.

The news is interesting but sad. Give yourself a break and go inside to an inner journey instead.

The less attractions you have now the more you'll have MASS attractions later--see it that way.

Leaving a small town was leaving a prison. Relocation pulled me outa the hell of false accusations.

Your loving liberal feminist sister was a communist, loving Bernie Sanders and Pocahontas.

DISTRACT FROM NEWS

Let music evoke thought, not the news. The mind is tracked: watch carefully who's your muse.

If all your life you wanted their love and now you're old but rich and they're sniffing you out?

Block them & the thought. Think of Jerry Lewis who disinherited 5 sons: not a nickel to a liberal.

CHAOS & ROT PREFACE

No respect to man unless husband. You've made gods outa people/self-esteem long gone.

It tortures me the more I know of Ukraine and Afghanistan like I'm taking the world on.

Stop divulging your inner emotions to strangers--a clear sign you're still unboundaried to danger.

Your show of emotions even crying is like blood in the water and the sharks will quickly gather.

KEEP THINGS IN FAMILY/STOP BLABBING

Keep things within your family and be smart from now on. You blab so much, dirty laundry shown.

When he calls don't talk so much about yourself. I know you're alone & ignored but don't show it gal.

The minute someone gives attention it all pours out--years of not being heard or cared about.

Don't do this, be smart this time. Don't let unfinished business of past ruin it with this new guy.

I figure I've written it all down, I'm not gonna bore him with it too. Just read my books around.

I figure I've written it all down, I'm not gonna bore him with it too. Just read my books if he wants to.

I know you don't wanna be 90 but it's the highest stage when we're at our highest apex see.

The skin may shrivel up and the body recede but the temporal lobes BURST open to eternity.

At this highest sagacious eldering stage, an elder has a panoramic view and can see eternity.

CHAOS & ROT PREFACE

Any man complements her and she goes wild giving him everything. It's common, I saw it happening.

Retirement is like slipping on cozy pajamas. No more deadlines, making nice or putting up with ya.

Retirement is taking naps when you want or being totally alone to finally discover who you are.

Retirement--eldering--is falling outa structure into a new world of inner discovery without censure.

Not putting up with people anymore is the biggest thing. You won't believe the release that brings!

SO YOU MADE A FOOL OF YOURSELF

You made a dam fool of yourself, said terrible things even a horrible monster--it's all erased sir.

No more office politics, dealing with socialist freaks or that cowering kowtowing to bosses see.

Elders were respected in all traditional cultures and given the first seat in the senate for sure.

In the west esp America they're given inferior status--a sense of obsolescence is put upon us.

It's a crying shame because from elders comes essential knowledge to be passed on and gained.

That's all prevented now there's no respect and they're put away as useless eaters liberals say.

But they don't give a dam, they die without notice except the will time and that's atrocious.

What made them hate Christianity: anyone could have God in them: slave, servant or leper see.

CHAOS & ROT PREFACE

It reversed everything on the elites vs. who they saw as upstarts. It became an upside down world.

Mothers speaking out are the terrorists but a black supremacist shooting 10 people isn't.

Evil is a deprivation. It's the absence of existence and being so will always collapses on its own.

How peaceful and safe my little country neighborhood vs. what's going on around the world.

SAD SISTER STORIES

Some were complicitous--going along to get along--and some were bystanders who didn't oppose at all.

The truth is coming out about sibling abuse. Our recovery is speaking out about it too.

Sibling abuse is least reported but is larger than spousal and child abuse combined [it's morbid].

It has consequences way into adulthood similar to parent-child abuse, to this I can attest.

Up to 80% of siblings experience some form of maltreatment and the therapy is to report this.

Sibling abuse has been called the "forgotten abuse" and this silencing is the biggest problem too.

There are forty million sibling abuse survivors--let that sink in to realize this silent childhood torture.

Underreported sibling abuse goes under the radar. The rivalry is reciprocal, the motive attention.

It starts as little children but escalates into full blown sibling abuse carrying on thru the years.

CHAOS & ROT PREFACE

WHEN RIVALRY BECOMES ABUSE

The problem is when sibling rivalry becomes sibling abuse: the intent to harm and control Sue.

The abuse is not a periodic incident but a repeated pattern going on in decades of torture.

In most cases early rivalry carries on into adulthood with emotional savagery and career inability.

One is aggressor, the other feels disempowered. There is bullying with motive to hurt every hour.

Usually the older dominates the younger, pushing them around. They gossip to the whole town.

It is quite serious and also criminal since a sister will destroy everything about you: ALL.

The reason for abuse is to establish superiority and provoke fear/distress in the other see.

It's the power of imbalance causing the pain see. I was so frustrated controlled by dummies.

The abuser is most judgmental. Tickle torture becomes physical force later as in an intervention.

EXTREME JEALOUSY IS COMMON

Extreme sibling jealousy is common becoming increasingly more destructive as time goes on.

There is retaliation after the abused sets healthy boundaries. Get ready for this quickly.

When setting boundaries smear campaigns arise quickly because they can't stand you winning.

CHAOS & ROT PREFACE

The abusers lie, steal and cheat their kin. In the will signing they'll do everything to exclude em.

The older sisters spread rumors and ruin the reputation of their sibling, spilling the beans to anybody.

Flying monkeys: They have their friends gang up on their sibling and it's traumatic/sickening.

Flying monkeys bribed to gang up on siblings has ended in beatings and even rape, no kidding.

They recruit flying monkeys to bully and STALK their sibling, to spy on every little thing.

They will steal the trust fund or inheritance from the sibling, employing lawyers to cripple em.

SISTER ABUSE AND PANIC ATTACKS

They do bad things to punish the target. To not invite to important occasions and make it obvious.

The survivors suffer with negative symptoms and medical conditions, like thirty of them.

This is not what's wrong with you, it's about what HAPPENED to you from sibling abuse.

Panic attacks, eating disorders, addictions of all kinds, constant anxiety and nightmares, aye.

Fear of the dark, insomnia and autoimmune conditions like Multiple Chemical Sensitivity [MCS].

Adverse childhood experiences [ACE] becomes codependency as adult, that's logical.

The stages of recovery from sibling abuse require the victim to NAME what happened: do it.

CHAOS & ROT PREFACE

We're releasing Traumatic Amnesia. Denial and lost memory is a predictable sign of trauma.

Stop denying the truth now and speak up about sibling abuse destroying your youth and goals.

Educate yourself on sibling abuse. It is healing, therapeutic and builds your self-confidence.

90% of the abusers deny and lie about abusing their siblings and never take accountability.

JEALOUS CHRISTIAN SIBLINGS

Jealousy in Christian siblings too has been going on since the beginning, see Abel and Cain.

Just because she's Christian doesn't mean she's not jealous in fact many times it's opposite.

Cain murdered his brother because Abel received God's favor. Nothing shows the dynamics better.

Jealousy is not the characteristic of a godly person and it's hell on this earth to live with one.

Toxic Christian siblings: there's nothing new under the sun, you will be betrayed by all of them.

I prayed over my toxic siblings and God put the story of Joseph on my broken heart for healing.

Joseph was betrayed by his siblings who were jealous of his wonderful gifts anointed by God see.

They were jealous of his special dreams and visions--his obvious anointing by the Lord, see friends?

Joseph's brothers set out to trick him and then sell him into slavery. Just imagine the treachery.

CHAOS & ROT PREFACE

Then his evil brothers turned around and told the father Joseph had been killed. Malicious people.

Moral of this lesson: He went to the palace from prison and thus everything evens out in the end.

Years later his siblings begged for forgiveness and they all reconciled, so that's the end, aye.

SIGNS OF TOXICITY IN CHRISTIAN SIBLINGS

Many claim to be Christian but are often pathological liars and wolves in sheep's clothing.

False Christians are excessively prideful with false humility, showing no fruits of the spirit see.

They bully you, they spy on you and have a mobbing mentality—it's ALL of us against you see.

They delight in your pain and suffering. It's hard to realize they take great pleasure in it ok.

The spirit of envy and jealousy takes deep root. A stronghold keeps them bound up/yoked too.

It's rare we see false Christians actually take ownership of a critical spirit and harsh judgements.

Toxic siblings neglect to protect you and will not defend you. You're on your own sister, adieu.

Any of the others who condone the toxic abuser is equally abusive, that's central to healing.

Sly, covert, malicious and toxic: these are wolves in sheep's clothing, not Christians in their walk.

The mask wearers are superficial and inauthentic and they do not have the Fruit of the Spirit.

LIBERAL CHAOS & ROT

The victims are the invaders, not the homeowners? When government gets involved things get reversed.

Cancel Culture nuts: In the name of diversity, it's uniformity. In the name of tolerance, its intolerance.

Hated whiteness: Individualism, hard work, objectivity, family, progress, sense of urgency, delayed gratification.

They're Marxists. I believe in equal opportunity/guns they believe in gov-assured equal outcome/no guns.

As Christians we believe love is the answer but we wanna be well-armed just in case--that's so obvious.

They were primed (dumbed down) in the schools. The youth know nothing and just wanna be cool.

The question is: why did they hate me? Cuz I was in sin using anxiety-avoiding devices to adapt to THEM.

Old Bohemian saying: The dragon must die. It means good must triumph over evil right before our eyes.

Narcissistic self-indulgent Millennials, who needs em. They don't seem to appreciate anything, avoid em.

They're like kittens who want to be loved but pull back in terror of being hurt. Be sweet and just endure.

CRITICISM IS NOT RACISM

Criticism is not racism darnit. Get a life and start investigating true reality not your warped vision of whodunit.

Narcissistic traits: arrogance, self-centeredness, a sense of entitlement, lacking empathy, being manipulative.

Communal narcissism: motivated by approval/attracting attention by being more altruistic than anyone.

LIBERAL CHAOS & ROT

We see ugly competitiveness and aggression when communal narcissists become pro-social.

There's **TWO** kinds of intelligence: that which sees what is missing and that seeing what is needed.

Tho' it sounds funny in this generation, the worst thing about divorce is a female losing a man's protection.

The world treats you totally differently if you're a married woman. It was like a miracle of nature, amen?

Having your face pushed in the mud is learning and overcoming disrespect is experience, the best.

Born with so much Scottish pride I had to exert every ounce of energy to overcome the snide.

It wasn't that I was outwardly "conservative" but that I wouldn't conform--they hated my independence.

It wasn't that they hated short hair, just my independence at choosing it--they gaslight to feel one UP.

What I went thru in a small liberal desert town in California was my Ph.D. in the Streets from unloving cheats.

The cops were horrible too since liberalism implies tyranny and a police state--not like Mayberry.

ME AGAINST THE VISCIOUS MOB

It was me against the vicious mob for twenty years but then I got married and I was left standing there.

Some women marry for provision, some for protection and I was a lucky one he was also a friend.

To be a single woman in small liberal desert town surrounded by mountains with no escape, hey.

Young men, old men--it didn't matter, get the f outa here! I just wanna be alone but they wouldn't hear.

LIBERAL CHAOS & ROT

And then I got married and the seas parted and I was ALONE at last and he always allowed it.

It was just like prince gave me escape from two older evil sisters in cahoots with drunk mother.

But then if I were to lose the prince's love, he'd regress back with the sisters, bribed to hate her.

WIN A MAN'S PROTECTION

It's all a system and you'd better stay whole to be on top of one or endure the Fallen Hero Syndrome.

I once read Beethoven lived in a small town where the children would ridicule and beat him.

Well I was invaded by a gang of boys--children in adult bodies--and no one would protect me.

Finally a church took me to town to get a restraining order and it was all over. Life really sux without a lover.

Two wings or two separate houses, that's the only way some wives can live without symptoms.

I've worked all my life to get to here and cannot adapt to anyone anymore, that's called LEISURE.

Cuz it's interruption in the flow, it stops what I know as a thinker, ruminator, dreamer, pearl seeker.

For a woman to say she doesn't need a man is really insane. We need them or life's a dreary rain.

MARITAL FIGHTING IS UGLY/PRESUMPTUOUS

It helps to know marital fighting is ugly and temporary insanity. I'd never do that again, really.

To think what God has to look down at with people like us. We're all sinners, there's no one good Jesus says.

LIBERAL CHAOS & ROT

It's when someone abuses verbally or acts like he's gonna hit you so you reject him and he acts like the victim.

THE CULPRITS PLAY VICTIM

These are called Presumptuous Sins. They presume too much on the relationship: step back or face ruin.

But with you and me it would be clean since it's a sealed bond with God-- in other words it's not of this world.

The younger man is attracted to her clarity, lack of game playing and the fact that she knows herself.

I've been there, done that, had enough of it. I just want tranquility in our home with you and the cats.

Married, I could just do what I wanted for once! Single, it was like I was constantly fighting resistance [enigma?]

I wanna be protected by a strong man so I can just do what I want! You've got each other trained, no one else.

Tho' he never reads my work, he's my patron just by being there and keeping my head above water man.

I think of you all day long, my destiny. Everything goes thru that filter--it enlarges me to where I wanna be.

Destiny just moves into place unthinkingly--an uncontrollable force of nature full of meaning.

Life should end at a climax--APEX--not a slow descent into disrepair, feeling obsolete and then madness.

DESTINY is an inexorable force of nature it seems as things just change and move into perfect place.

Not only does God eventually get gossips for their calumny but anyone who would listen to them/your enemy.

AOC appeals to urban poor and intellectual white. I get how they go together but are they really that tight?

LIBERAL CHAOS & ROT

AMERICA BEGAN AS PURITANS

America began on Calvinism [puritanism] and this affected laws and everything else, mostly attitude.

Total Depravity--describing man--was so ingrained and thus in the Old West everyone even kids had guns.

God doesn't choose/love everyone--that is LIMITED Election. As He chooses, we must also vet EVERYONE.

God does NOT love everyone and it's the Armenian Heresy that He does. He hated Esau/workers of iniquity.

New church/pagan new age sees man as good not depraved, and as all-loving God despite how we misbehave.

The clear man is relieved to know man is totally depraved, when he views his sinful past it is all explained.

The modern church won't talk of man's sinfulness, it just comes too close--but it's all about repentance.

In sin, we miss our mark--DESTINY, achievement. With repentance we hit the mark in prefect grace.

Having found our predestined groove God designed before our birth, He perseveres to the end of our years.

So watch out for people cuz few are chosen and the rest are still depraved. You can really see it in this age.

THE MODERN CHURCH IS ANTI-CALVINIST

Most churches/psych paradigms are anti-Calvinist: saying man is good and God is all-loving--DAM LIES.

Limited Election offends them since it doesn't seem fair. Like everyone goes to heaven in the hereafter.

They can't stand not believing that God loves them in spite of their filthy sins or that they're good in any case.

LIBERAL CHAOS & ROT

Jesus said "don't call me good, only God is good." The social narcissist wants to be seen as the most nicest.

Women are not to preach OR call themselves motivational speakers with a Christian background.

Bible says women are not to educate men. I'm thinking that's because they so easily slip into paganism.

Whether it's the modern church or the feminist, they hate hearing about how totally depraved they are.

Man's default setting is total depravity, only God brings him up to decency. This is why we are separate you see.

I don't have to make up demons to justify how I acted, it's my default setting to be totally obnoxious.

Only God draws you out of the deep dark cultural abyss, the muddy waters you swam in and couldn't resist.

Picasso, Einstein and Frank Lloyd Wright never slept but just took catnaps. That's how I'm doing it in fact.

Take away basic rights and replace with faux rights--transgender bathrooms-- and give USA last rites.

"The nations will ask: Why hath the Lord done this to their land? Was He that angry?" Yes, absolutely.

LET EM ALL IN: LIBS WANT OPEN BORDERS

I love *legal* immigration--I think it's wonderful. People must do the work to come here and make it legal.

People who condone illegal immigration are enemies cuz we're being killed in 300 sanctuary cities.

Liberals wanna let em all in--do they ever think of what it's doing to small towns, my friends?

Progressives want NO borders, they think it's good. But we're losing our ways and livelihoods.

LIBERAL CHAOS & ROT

Cloward and Piven: They're gonna let in the masses, all on the dole--then pull the plug for all.

It was such a bad deal for us, not for them. We gave everything away--all our leverage too, gone.

Iran was such a bad deal it just makes me sick. We had far more power before--what finks.

It was such a bad deal--we gave it all away. What a laughing stock we are in the world today.

Legal immigrants want border security too--it's just common sense. They're not dense, they want defense.

The nations see the results of profligate sins, though we don't. In every case respect is lost--dethroned.

There's an end to the gravy train when people ungratefully turn their back on Thee with disdain.

Please Father heal our wonderful country and land. Bring us back to freedom, how we began.

We were in a whirlwind--the fastest things had ever changed. It was scary, overwhelming, deranged.

Foes: Those who want to kill us got 150 billion bucks and the nuclear bomb.
Thanks a lot Obama you bum.

THE LEFT LOVES RADICAL ISLAM

The controlled left loves radical Islam. Can you believe that? They even help them get a bomb.

It just can't be a conspiracy to get Donald in so he can flip flop and we're screwed again.

Donald are you just a ringer to get us excited only to hand it over to that RINO Ryan later?

It was a more decent time: conservative and fine. These traditionals knew where to draw the line.

LIBERAL CHAOS & ROT

You say you'll put up the border, kill ISIS, bring jobs back and defund China but is this more poli-trivia?

The youth are purposely kept in the dark. They don't see ISIS as sharks and they love Barack.

We've got to see what Americana means to you and me: freedom from this awful tyranny.

Americans are so dense being politically correct we face the end of our country with out defense!

In our crazy world loss is gain, slavery is freedom, killing is blessing and stealing is helping.

They created a Tower of Babel: total confusion, contradiction and chaos intended to break our will.

How to drive people crazy so they're of none effect: contradict and create chaos in the Elect.

They purposely contradict themselves constantly because that's Rules for Radicals by Saul Alinsky.

Youth tend to be more idealistic but that's ridiculous as they force us into deadly impotence.

SCIENCE FICTION WOULD MAKE MORE SENSE

It's like science fiction but that'd make more sense. We're falling into destruction, immense.

They wanted us all poor save an elite top. They got the red carpet/grandeur and we got the slop.

The contradictions made us feel panicky cuz it meant tyranny: helpless cuz he wouldn't fight ISIS.

The professors all look the same: jeans, black shirt and hateful of America's values (mentally lame).

To take down Mt. Rushmore--can we stand anymore? They intend to delete our history to it's core.

LIBERAL CHAOS & ROT

The blatant contradictions/coldness made us panicky/helpless cuz they wouldn't stop but God blessed.

Will Donald save Christians? Will he be resolute and label those who want to kill us (vermin)?

What we need is someone who cannot be bought. That's how the whole system works, a lot.

Go Trump after this hump of the worst president ever who thinks he's a hunk but in truth, junk.

Green police tyranny (banning things) is pure piracy and just a way to get our currency.

We all have the same problem though they seek to divide: tyranny as our freedoms have died.

A LIBERAL TOWN IS HORRIBLE

Living in a liberal town was horrible but at least I learned what youth are taught in the schools.

Now this is pure class. He tells the truth and so the powers hate him though they're the dumbass.

There's an arrogance and conceit that comes over people when they're confirmed by evil.

Most psychology should be called Social Science cuz it all comes down to interactional defiance.

If anyone here loved previous president please leave this group. Cuz no one could be that dumb, or stoop.

Rigging elections and breaking laws is on the democrats, ya'll.

Most of shootings happen in democratic areas of gun control and also where poverty prevails.

Please spread the word that HIllary's gotten weird and if she gets in there's much to be feared.

This woman is a sick feminist and very vindictive. False accusations reign in colleges. Witches!

LIBERAL CHAOS & ROT

Superior man defends the weak: babies, elderly, pets. Pro-choicers have no heart, without regrets.

In Islam the canine is not allowed. And 100,000 Muslims arrive each month-- too bad for the dog.

Gun confiscation is ruthless to elderly who more than anyone else must be able to defend themselves.

GIVE UP HALF-TRUTH FOX: FOUND TIME!

When I gave up FOX (half-truths/liberalism) I got 12 hours daily of newly found time, amen!

Women after abortions: heartsick or hard as nails: angry, embittered, mean, evil thoughts and smells.

Democrats are evil because of what they believe in: it's a 12-plank program like abortion and open borders man.

Gay Gestapo: Just like the militant homo network that took over Nazi Germany long ago.

Going from "responsibility" to "rights" everything changed. Simultaneously women got deranged.

Cowards, traitors, perverts, murderers, the immoral, magicians, idol-worshippers and liars.

Many liberals are well-dressed and articulate but it's still the ideology of total destruction, imminent.

He's a hero to the herd with out morals. From his slick innuendoes they use violence to settle quarrels.

They could SWAT me tonight for speaking against the perversion of 5 year olds. Lord, we've been sold!

After years of feeling secure we reached a point where no one was safe. We all felt it (like expecting a raid.)

LIBERAL CHAOS & ROT

Total confusion is the new reality, so keep sanity by seeing the blasphemy/how they act callously.

If NBC is 10% true and CNN is 20% true and FOX is 50% true--why waste time with any—eschew.

1. Turn your life from casual (drop ins) to formal (no friends). 2. Now be open to holy spirit (be kingpins).

Donald is the real deal, kids. Get your head out of Hollywood images so they don't make you helpless, forbid.

They don't say they're equal, "gays are superior". There's a whole list of ways, just like Hitler.

You can feel the pressure everywhere. It's brutal, arguing is futile, free thinkers punished--need prayer.

It used to be God but now Satan's in control of men's minds. Divide from them, stick to the refined.

SOAPS PORTRAY MORALISTS AS PSYCHOTIC

Soaps are portraying moralists as psychotic, paranoid nuts. Meanwhile, they normalize the klutz.

That's what liberals do: invite a bunch of people to your house. They impose things on you of course.

Ideologies are the problem, rather than adapting point-by-point constrained by the constitution.

Liberals run the media/universities so we think there are more than there are (a minority, sub-par).

America is now invaded by an army of foreigners but also minds warped by seeing through blinders.

The nightmare America had become under that monster must be told, to the devil we were sold.

LIBERAL CHAOS & ROT

Obama's army was immigrant youth. The "dreamers" arrived and went right on the dole, that's the truth.

California is banning travel to America: eight states not part of the swamp which is mostly there.

Let their anger do themselves in, let their wrath give you victory. The left is collapsing and we're not sorry.

Corruption and nonsensical ideology: That's the left in control over us with out apology.

The saints have a stinging conscience and that's what distinguishes them from the dumb masses.

It's called inversion (enontiodromia) when they get theirs. This is revolution:
no more tears!

People will get their come-uppins so just wait a little while then they're gone, good riddance.

THEIR SIN WILL BE SHOUTED FROM THE ROOFTOPS

Like a thread unraveling a sweater, it's all gonna come out! What they did to us, losing our clout.

The anti-genius forces were "tolerant" BS learned in schools: To demoralize us--a deliberate move.

Schools became a way controlling minds by tracking them into gutter grooves and global designs.

If you accept their crap it means your identity has been eclipsed by another = stormy weather.

All their ridiculous and un-natural notions are peer-maintained. They work each other up, in the main.

The new age is "hangout" culture. That's the goal, not accomplishing great things but conforming to vulgar.

LIBERAL CHAOS & ROT

Don't waste precious time on dumb pursuits and subjects. You see we're goin' down and no one objects.

Then what is freedom? It is the will to be responsible to ourselves. Friedrich Nietzsche

A free society is one where it is safe to be unpopular. Adlai Stevenson

You're too ego-driven. Selfies--all about you/empty stuff--while barbarians enter in aiming for killin'

Stop this shame, bud. You got dirty from living in mud and that's why the prince became a dud.

Jesus is in control over evil things if you don't get involved with the world (like having flings).

When in fear of foes, keep reading Psalms. You will have victory--God's words are like bombs!

TV: WIMPS PORTRAYED AS DUMB INGRATES

Men are so bruised from being wimped in this culture: fodder for scammers who know their number.

The inner self hates things you're staying around. Evil spirits can degrade and they confound.

Facebook/TV is so petty compared to what God has to give. With TV news my mind is a sieve.

TV keeps you from the right-brain. Anything that tracks the mind obstructs creative gains.

You must confront lasciviousness in your kids. Make them yours, not his-- Satan and the abyss.

Dark upstarts: soul-less creatures mimicking the social realm and sickening to be around.

LIBERAL CHAOS & ROT

Sun/Moon gods and guardian angels instead of going to Jesus the head honcho, the most special.

Rather than hating their guts, pray for those in authority over you and that there will be few.

They did it because they could: mean and underhanded, it's hard to forget those hearts of wood.

The solution to unfair accusation is to retreat, regroup (get the scoop) then attack with facts.

Those who vote decide nothing, those who count the vote decide everything. Joseph Stalin

WHEN YOUR WORLD HATES YOUR GUTS

When your world hates your guts but since you're mentally ill you don't see it, that's being a klutz.

The Wife of the Alcoholic Syndrome: she gets far crazier than him with her own drinking binge.

Never belittle your man. The most important note to woman vs. those of feminist vermin.

What is it about Christians that makes em hate their guts? God's in us but the devil's in nuts.

How fascinating the forces of human society: poli-sci, sociology, psychology and systems theory.

I know them, though I loathe them. It's me vs. the whole tribe--trust no man, have no friends.

Pet peeve: First things don't add up then you question further and they evade or have to leave.

After attacks there was lassitude, passivity and annoyance in O's voice-- we accepted this crap, no choice.

LIBERAL CHAOS & ROT

She's a fantastic homemaker/lady and he's a genius/gentleman. Get some respect, amen.

Instead of "how could they do this to me" say "they know not what they do, it's the devil's crew."

You who work for the system make a mint in pensions but they'll eventually kill you too man.

I'm going to where people are still sane—to the red mountains, the familial and religious county of Kane.

Things they believed in I did not and they hated me for it--that's why the rejection, so forget it.

Monica Lewinsky making a mint from speaking engagements about public shaming, huh?

INFIDELITY OVERLOAD & FEMINIST TOADS

Infidelity Overload: Women being brainwashed into promiscuity even more than men, amen.

Be ye perfect: Must repent but few churches instruct the truth. Be good to be blessed.

'Go Topless Day' is the new feminist thing yet they get mad when we stop and stare--is it fair?

In high school the buxom women were the most popular. How udder-ly ridiculous/improper.

There is always death/disease to those breaking God's laws. This slows sin down from the cause.

The Clinton Foundation is a slush fund for grifters and a vehicle to facilitate massive bribers.

We're all sinners, even them--it's a matter of repentance. But they still condemn, relentless.

LIBERAL CHAOS & ROT

Love and light won't help you. The only beneficial is Jesus and also facing your dark shadow.

When I saw her I was in disbelief. 20 years of anti-depressants and feminism stole life like a thief.

I hate liberals cuz they're immoral and I was immoral when I was a liberal.

She was so emotionally needy that any man who was a tad bit nice she'd plan to marry--that's insanity.

SICK IN THE GUT—GONE TOO FAR

When you feel sick you know it's gone too far. The system is an anachronism now--block to be a star.

Stick to your age group or just conservatives. This divide is too wide, don't waste time and stay refined.

You've come too far/worked to hard. Don't fall back to below par, cut em loose and open to destiny, star!

The un-family is a black cloud. Move into loving/encouraging others now, time is limited so say it loud.

Left got so weird I conflated to all liberals I know and cut em loose to find the True Self and now I'll show.

The greatest cartoon maker's not cute and magical but sad, perverted, deceptive and tragical.

Political correctness is maintained by fear of being a social outcast if we don't--see this, reject it.

Lost morals in the female bring on relationship hate. When men run towards purity she gets irate.

Movie directors resort to effects and they use sex cuz it's from lost genius and the sin-hex.

Not all the same, libs: Yin and Yang, black and white, love and hate, morals vs tolerance.

LIBERAL CHAOS & ROT

WE NEED STRONG LEADERS

We need someone with a strong temperament who is fast. Jeb, Hil and the rest would never last.

Trump's the best, he's got the juice. He'll get along well with Putin cuz they both know the truth.

They'd always lay evil seeds against me so anyone I worked with as trustee was hostile, see?

Heaven is a cozy cabin in the wilderness and hell is disorder and chaos in the city mess.

Some churches are run by the devil himself. Be careful whom you are around and ignore siren sounds.

Just like Nazi Germany, a political movement has divided families: sister against brother and other tragedies.

Her bitching chips away and then suddenly he's history and she wonders why? Steeped in misery.

WICKED MEN HYPNOTIZING WEAK WOMEN IN THEIR HOMES

The police will not protect you in California. That's why I left, it's a wonder I'm still here with ya'.

I don't want em coming here, stealing stuff and sayin what they're sayin. Cut em loose, you'll be flying.

Work, then relax. Go into your magic right brain, remove the world's hex: the good life, at last.

They're just a bunch of dumbasses who do not care. They'll self-destruct soon but you have flair.

For happy homelife women should be in the home to prepare nutritious food and feed the pets.

LIBERAL CHAOS & ROT

We all know you don't control bullies by being nice to them. We need to resist and fight back, amen.

MUST MANAGE PEOPLE AND BULLIES

More than half of females are taking SRI's--thinking they're "happy pills"--and some even kill.

If they're acting the herd script they'll make fools of themselves, not speak truth as magic elves.

Speak the truth about anti-depressants--they're not happy pills. The victim's never happy just ill.

The joy and sense of cornucopia is the right-brain--which SRI's block--and so they're a loss not a gain.

Proof that God exists is seen all around. But not to the sinner, he/she just wants to be big in town.

Out of respect for critics, you're filled with remorse. Lose respect, repent and you're back on the horse.

Respecting your foes is Stockholm Syndrome. Lose respect and you'll grow (not look like a gnome).

Everywhere you look, boobs in your face. Shameless brazen cleavage come back to reality, please.

I don't wanna have your meetings that cost me money when I don't even need your advice honey.

You gotta know all the rules to break em. What is genius: sparks bypassing all that's been learned.

Been scammed by three geeks who wouldn't just do what I asked. They're dumbed/can't multi-task.

This isn't medicine. I'm afraid of the whole creepy profession. I'll never trust any of em again.

LIBERAL CHAOS & ROT

Sure there are some good doctors, but by and large it's a drugging thing now not prevention.

The "music" is the kinda noise you hear in stores. It's this cheap, corny contrived crap I deplore.

AVOID WEAK PEOPLE & LIMP HANDSHAKES

Limp handshakes smell cuz there's no moral strength to always do what's right and they go to hell.

I was raised a Calvinist and very modest so it's doctor's exams I detest (seems like I was molested).

Facebook is our work since that's the vehicle for spreading the word that we're no longer first.

New Age acts like the greatest accomplishment is to just hang out-- blocking the creative spout.

The bible says not to pierce or paint our bodies as the heathen do. It's inferior so ask: why do you?

Most marital arguments come from a false feminist narrative--they bitch and whine like it's imperative.

Due to the False Feminist Narrative (FFN) wives pick fights--and in just this way they ruin life.

Just when things are tranquil she rises up in anger. It's strange how systems work (danger).

My husband is a great problem-solver. Any mess I have he fixes so to hell with feminist detractors.

Women think it's chic to degrade husbands. They've been told it's intellectual, can you imagine?

Separate from culture, you march to a different drummer and it makes you different like a foreigner.

LIBERAL CHAOS & ROT

Hell is a place where there is no reason. If that's your friends or family don't discuss politics or it's treason.

It doesn't matter that he doesn't know anything. It's the intention of his heart that saves us underlings.

People lost the ability to think. They do technical things like pilot planes but it's still a herd: rinky-dink.

Just bcuz we have the right to dress that way doesn't mean we should. Brazen women = hearts of wood.

DEMONS FROM PREVIOUS MARRIAGES

He had a demon in him from a previous marriage and as it all came out at her she became disparaged.

I don't wanna take my time refuting them. They're so low that only degrades my consciousness, man.

Family scapegoats suffer the most in trust funds. Discrimination by jealous housewives is no fun.

How you're held down by how they see you: Trying to get approval or change their minds = pooh!

The first few years of marriage it's The Taming of the Shrew then once adapted you're one not two.

Dumbed-down dudes: chumps who just wanna be petted, have their egos soothed and told platitudes.

You're supposed to love your husband whether you do or not--so just do it:
enjoy the knot.

A good woman is broken like a horse then he'll give her all she wants of course.

Computers are our life, we have to do this: Sit here all day and night despite being dissed.

LIBERAL CHAOS & ROT

They're not Christians: they're always searchin' and know nothing about redemption.

Never forget the wicked will always fall: Though they walk tall soon they're gone and that's all.

If you're blind, dead and dumb it's a wonderful world as you party on never worried (numb).

They'res nothing so unattractive in a woman as a seared conscience: gross, lost, no finesse.

UNATTRACTIVE WOMEN HAVE SEARED CONSCIENCES

There's nothing so unattractive in a woman as a seared conscience: gross, lost, no finesse.

Foul: Stinking, loathsome, extremely dirty; indecent, profane, wicked, abominable, stormy.

Only seared consciences could go along with something like this and it shows who you are, sis.

Now's the time to not sink in their swill. Stop focusing on the ephemeral and in-fill.

As my mother used to say "swill!" That's all they are so stay above those who steal/kill.

He ruined an old lady--He siphoned off from the family budget to his buddies.

Empty hedonistic mindlessness becomes emptier very quickly and one looks ugly/sickly.

ISOLATION IS THE BEST PROTECTION

Most people want security in this world, not liberty. Henry Louis Mencken

If the choice is a nice house in a neighborhood or a shack alone in nature, I'll take the latter.

LIBERAL CHAOS & ROT

Take the best from the shabby past then put em in a new cast = destiny--
and what a blast.

The best self-protection is isolation. Have friends for pillars but notice
your aversions.

Give me the liberty to know, to utter, and to argue freely according to
conscience, above all liberties. John Milton

Freedom is never an achieved state; like electricity, we've got to keep
generating it or the lights go out. Wayne LaPierre

When everyone is thinking the same, no one is thinking. John Wooden

A slave is he who cannot speak his thoughts. Euripides

A real man always does all he says he'll do and what he predicts always
comes true.

Though I'm glad the BLM owns Utah land cuz the gorgeous red cliffs
would be filled with houses man.

Education is a better safeguard of liberty than a standing army. Edward
Everett

When the same man, or set of men, holds the sword and the purse, there
is an end of liberty. George Mason

If freedom of speech is taken away then dumb and silent we may be led
like sheep to the slaughter. George Washington

To change masters is not to be free. Jose Perez

You can chain me, you can torture me, you can even destroy this body,
but you will never imprison my mind. Gandhi

If liberty means anything at all, it means the right to tell people what
they don't want to hear. George Orwell

NO LIBERTY IN THE CRAZY CITIES

LIBERAL CHAOS & ROT

Guard with jealous attention the public liberty. Suspect every one who approaches that jewel. Patrick Henry

Liberty is meaningless where the right to utter one's thoughts and opinions (the dread of tyrants) has ceased to exist. Frederick Douglass

Make men wise, and by that very operation you make them free. William Godwin

The man who does not do his own thinking is a slave, and is a traitor to himself and his fellow men. Robert G. Ingersoll

The history of liberty is a history of the limitations of governmental power not the increase of it. Woodrow Wilson

Where liberty is, there is my country. Benjamin Franklin

Liberty is rendered even more precious by the recollection of servitude

The natural progress of things is for liberty to yield and government to gain ground. Thomas Jefferson

Enough of us prayed so God sent Donald Trump: God intervened in our affairs to survive this slump.

LOUSY LASCIVIOUS LIBERALS

They've become horrible from the things they believe in. Not born that way, it's just psychology of sin.

Increasingly we're judged by what group we're in not what we produce-- that means thuggery, of course.

It's not over till it's over—we could return from the brink. With Trump we triumph/end this stink.

Trump-hating liberals are lizards in fact and it's cuz we may never get our freedoms back.

Politicians get used to the perks and settle in--yes sir--until everything they do is the worst.

LIBERAL CHAOS & ROT

When they bash Trump just keep saying "he didn't say that" cuz he didn't and you know it.

Many would-be actors end up as news anchors and they dumbly mimic false narratives.

How much can we take of these naked girls on FOX? Avoid this boring and tedious paradox.

For all my hatred of the enemy I have so much love for everyone else and that's victory.

Hillary: the third term of the Barry O man-child administration and for sure end of the nation.

A billion to bring Trump down and the kids are believing it. He's a nice man but they aren't seein' it.

NARRATIVE CONTROLLED BY LEFT

Marches behind social justice while protecting it's own privileges: that's the liberal college.

Main media news (ruthless ambition without principals, dishonest and desperate) is smooth.

The ultra level trolling by the left is usually incendiary and ridiculous but Trump is always victorious.

The left wants to maintain it's privileges while they make us pay and aren't we sick of this?

The affluent left won't give up their homes to immigrants but make us do it--thanks.

Newspapers take direct orders from owners and that's what you're getting:
gophers.

Are we led by people who don't have a clue, or are they trashing us on purpose/making us blue?

LIBERAL CHAOS & ROT

Get this: Liberals hate low taxes/regulations, prosperity, and well-protected freedoms.

We've lost the American work ethic that made us great--a sad change into third rate.

The media is trying to divide this country while blaming Trump and supporters for it, ok?

WE MOVED TO A SAFER STATE, A FLY-OVER GREAT

We're moving to a safer state. Low regulations/taxes and right to self-defense make it great.

Trump is about Preserving and Expanding the American Dream while Ridding us of Fiends.

Trump subjects U.S. trade deals to a cost-benefit analysis vis-a-vis cold national interest.

Facts not ideology determine reality. So refuse to succumb to false narratives (silly).

You're not a free thinker, you mimic what you hear dear.

Trump may not be a great statesman but will surround himself with the best for his plans.

They're creating a mind control perception that Trump's going down--a trick, profound.

A billion to bring Trump down--that's why we're told this crap but our boy's still BIG in town.

If Mexico doesn't stop dumping criminals on us Trumps gonna come after them—big fuss.

Don't listen to anything Fox has to say. They've got an agenda so it's all bull, but hey...

LIBERAL CHAOS & ROT

We're told to look for covert racism wherever we go. This is just a mind-rape, you know.

If they're effective and tell the truth they're banned. That tells you who's in control and their plans.

Colbert is politically saying impeach the president. He's an actor and the head of this regiment.

The peace of society is obtained by force. Let God be avenger and He'll take care of you, of course.

Under Obama we said: Impeach the dumb leech or we're up a creek. The world is laughing so act, we beseech.

FEMINISTS LOVE HILLARY, GUILTY AS HELL

The democratic frontrunner Hillary Clinton "has to go to jail" and is "guilty as hell." Donald Trump

The pharisees would say "Oh, so unpresidential" because they're all phonies but so homicidal.

If you don't think she's guilty you're a complete psychotic zombie and buffoon living in a cocoon.

"Universal Basic Income" kills freedom/spirit, a welfare system like Indians confined to area/strata.

Postwar collapse of religion and growth of "me now" produced most petty and greedy generations: shallow.

Most spoiled, most entitled, most manipulative: greedy bullies and you can see it in your relatives.

As the most verbally abusive morally challenged generation goes into retirement we all pay for it.

Me-ism: When you get out of religion but retain mysticism.

LIBERAL CHAOS & ROT

The orgie of self-gratification lasting decades reflected in the financial scandals--it's the same.

All the rules of deferred gratification and the subjugation of desires to future goals were now gone.

This generation is (me now) sex freedom vs. the "repressed, self-hating self-over-regulating Puritans".

That so-called cosmic view of the universe is really merely the diminishing self under a curse.

With the fall of external rules there was no new development of internal rules.
Needed: jail for fools.

Punishment-based rules vs. learning-based principals acquired from years of desert solitude from y'all.

She wouldn't defer gratification for sake of others (stay in marriage) so children hurt/became abusers.

When there are no principals all that guides is immediate self-interest.

The arrested development from early fame creates a lack of intellectual depth from a bully pulpit.

STUDENTS FIT ONLY BY MOUTHING THE VISION

For students it's just easier to fit in mouthing that false vision.

Too many celebrities are spouting off political opinions and not providing quality entertainment.

Sixties Slide: Can't fire public school teachers, beginning a catastrophic decline in the west.

The principal (of not using force to get what you want) is absent also, and wow.

"Save and prepare" of previous generations, gone. Now it's the welfare state, greed, loving wrong.

LIBERAL CHAOS & ROT

Without thrifty principals you are bought off, in debt and bribed by political system for your allegiance.

You never cared about me, only those creepy people. You ended in a rest home and died, oh well.

Democrats have every incentive to split families since single moms vote democrat almost always.

Dems created conditions so single motherhood flourished despite lives destroyed/much anguish.

They all get testy but when you win you just forget about em. Don't hang on and don't fool with em!

THEY POOH-POOHED EVERYTHING I WANTED TO DO

Everything I wanted to do they would pooh-pooh. I'm so happy to be out from under: whew.

We're on the march and the empire is on the run. Don't get discouraged, Victory is fun.

The left has supported every enemy of America since the second world war-- that's just who they are.

Liberals say give up your culture, take mark of the beast, world government.

Maddow and professors are the priesthood and we're the devil cuz we see through hearts of wood.

Obama acting like he's still relevant when he's just another washed up liberal and arrogant.

Right decisions comes from God, liberals make em based on feelings, trends, popularity: flawed.

She was a sweet kid till she went off to college. Then she became crazy, debauched, my gosh...

LIBERAL CHAOS & ROT

Republicans talk like accountants but the left is always moral indictment-- more appeal to laymen.

Cult programming: "people of color"–though that's racism and they were the biggest slaveowners.

The left likes governments unresponsive to the people cuz the people are the problem--wow, how evil!

Left sees people as the problem cuz we don't like socialism. They're not for people/out to get you, ma'am.

They can't accept what we the people want so call it "resistance": angry, violent, arrogant.

In fear of called "racist" the cops slow-roll into black areas but more blacks killed in those instances.

LUNATIC LEFT HAS MONEY, POPULARITY AND INFLUENCE

They have money, popularity and influence but you're the best so hold your head up high for once.

The most disturbing thing of the century is the hyper-sexualization of childhood, truly. It's "Interesting, metro, cool".

Teaching weird sex to five year olds--trying to demoralize us then take control.

Boys are more emotional than girls but hide their feelings better. Think of that before being bitter.

Interesting, metro and cool or country clinger? One is going down and the other will be the winner.

The media's Russia psychosis is back and it's worse than ever. Hannity

The new age is so dark: life goes on and then it ends. Make something of your life by not following trends.

Feeling invincible is a form of make believe or possession: It's the major sign before utter ruin.

LIBERAL CHAOS & ROT

It all started in the sixties and the insane dumbness is seen in the progeny of these old hippies.

They believe in things false as though they were truths and their only religion is liberal, uncouth.

Thank you Lord for helping us put this one and only right man in the highest office, rid of the asses.

Trump is our only hope as we're on a tightrope between total disaster and prosperity faster.

Don't let failure you see all around (as we go down) determine your own cuz you've got God, hon'

LIBERAL LOGIC WORSE THAN CORRUPTION

We're split between socialism and corruption but the worst is in between: liberal logic since our teens.

Solution: Instill true family values in the people and train them in the bible to discern evil.

Liberal family members--what can be done? Nothing, son, it's no fun but they're just plain dumb.

Liberals wanna kill babies but let hardened criminals go. I don't like liberals and will tell them so.

Anyone can memorize misinformation (chant learning) but question: are they discerning?

Anger, hate, jealousy and fear is the psycho-spiritual posture and emotional palette of demons.

Insofar as the churches take on a polyanna all-good mentality they are just false religion and smilies.

We all have sins but that is definitely one of them. It is not superior as they say, amen.

LIBERAL CHAOS & ROT

Compensate with outer fluff not realizing nothing will fascinate as like your mind linked to God.

Women actually think they get power from dominating men and the sitcoms confirm that, amen.

In the context of past sick systems I feel shame but thinking of my friends and husband I feel the fame.

What a sad day in presidential history: that Obama could care less about something so gory.

Heart or heel: They either open their heart to you or you turn your heel on them: pooh.

THE WHOLE SYSTEM HATES ONE: TRIBALISM

They hated me--them and all their progeny. That's the way human systems work: like a Greek tragedy.

I don't accept your narrative: this contrived thing we have to learn by rote is weird and not admirable.

Don't listen to them and don't reply. A few jabs then walk away gently-- this is too low for you and I.

They're so dense don't waste any more time on them. Unfortunately some only learn by hitting bottom.

They hated first and then she sinned. Not the other way around: it was just self-medication.

The minute you explain yourself you're no longer the magic elf cuz you're obviously scared of them—hell!

She got haughty from riches, got like other witches and was never satisfied, constant itches.

Note the relation between poverty (being broke) and sex sin: it's prosperity vs. the trash bin.

LIBERAL CHAOS & ROT

The pets suffered the most when women left the next and for kids your staying home is best.

Look at the degraded lives with the woman out of the home. It's a fulltime job, never to roam.

Wives: It's all in the approach whether a man listens to you so be sweet and don't bitch.

Sure we should forgive–but it still builds faith to see them get theirs! God is justice/He cares!

There's something called holy hatred. it's justified at times as God hated those He humiliated.

Thank you Lord, for hating my enemies. I take you at your word and that solves all life's tragedies.

ANOMOLIES IN A SEPARATE REALITY/BLACK SHEEP

I come from a long line of anomalies in a separate reality from the mass: no conformity to the ass.

Calvinists know God does not love everybody, He hates–I would not adore Him were it not a reality.

Don't pray He'll stop the punishment on an enemy. It's for their own good, as they had wounded thee.

So your family never calls you--after this indifference/apathy why would you even want them to?

You got it, they don't. You were rewarded, they weren't. You are chosen by God, they aren't.

Superior men do not adapt to them--the underlings--but visa-versa and that's the way it is, yes sah.

Housekeeping is good exercise--you oughta try it sometime. Not protesting (small-time petty minds).

LIBERAL CHAOS & ROT

The average Joe has the attention span of a goldfish so they can't complete tasks, even if you ask.

The classic narcissus is so filled with self-loathing he must pretend he is the false self.

For years I lived with that sense of injustice. Good was bad, bad was good though I was the best.

Sinners lose all sense. They can't see how they appear--like asses--to the clear not the dense.

What makes humans different from animals? We can think (so shut up) not just eat/copulate.

You get bit after poking the bear but then they attack as a pack whether family or peer.

Great spirits have always encountered violent opposition form mediocre minds. Albert Einstein.

Mad at his first wife, he put his second through the ringer and that's called projection (a stinger).

Forget those sullied by your past sins. If you've repented but they can't forgive, good riddance.

REJECT JUNKARDS, SLOBS AND MESSERS (PORN ADDICTS)

I don't like your snippiness and messiness buddy and it all comes from pornography (being shady).

Studies have shown most men are into porn but they get away with it cuz it's a "European movie".

What do you think cleavages are? That's porn: In your face every day and you say its ok.

Don't think of the adversary anymore. It's a drag on consciousness and prevents God's abundant pour.

LIBERAL CHAOS & ROT

You say I'm corrupt yet you're all for the biggest criminals in history who are so out to lunch.

When phony feminism fails we see the Black Widow Spider Syndrome: her tyranny or breakdown.

Femininity is not about hair length. Get a buzzcut but be sweet, gentle and orderly (strength).

You must face your fear of disorder. God's not the author of confusion, which the good deplore.

Because of the evil things they believe in of course liberals are evil that's a no-brainer, people!

Elites trying to make us snap. Drive us so crazy and sick they can take over-- that's their map.

Hillary's comportment is "Madame Mao". Cold, cruel, entitled and arrogant-- worse than Obama, wow.

Weaklings are into power and thus they love seeing the enemies of their heroine/tyrant cower.

Hillary Clinton is a symbol of the hippies from the sixties. It's the end of an era, missy.

It's an end of an era! Praise God! Hillary Clinton must go to jail or it's a sign we've failed.

HILLARY AND THE HIPPIES FROM THE SIXTIES

Since you can see it you no longer have to defend it. It's part of your tissues and they will know it.

When he's in cash-control it's a slow dribble. But when I have it I start with a lot and end with a little.

It's not all about you, broad! Get over yourself, it's embarrassing and deeply flawed.

LIBERAL CHAOS & ROT

You're way above Fox News: filled with liberals omitting immigration and they seem obtuse.

If you want Sharia Law watch Saturday Night Live cheering our destruction which they minimize.

California is run by one man and it's totally liberal--lowest of the low and it's a line you must tow.

THEY TRIED TO WRECK THE COUNTRY

All these burdensome rules and regulations are just a way to usurp power as the rest of us cower.

By now everyone knows he tried to wreck the country and his cohort/third term was to be Hillary.

I've reached a point where I don't need the details of how the whole Western world is derailed.

Now neomasculine men (not metro sexual men) are just as rare as neofeminine females and it's sin.

Obama's daughters have a dozen armed guards while we're unprotected, sitting ducks seen as retards.

Slaves are regarded as the parasite class. That's why no one cares--we're beaten and sassed.

Even a preacher's son loses it through carnality (sensual appetites) when joy leaves and he enters the blight.

Government control of healthcare is just a way to force social programs on us and it's ruinous.

FOX is a scam showing just enough to be truth then diverting to the trivia--be done with them.

Liberals say "to hell with language/culture--let em all in": changing who we are forever, amen.

LIBERAL CHAOS & ROT

New America: brainwashed/drugged youth vote and foreign illegals who are not our friends.

Why are liberals resistant to borders and why are conservatives for it? Nazi guilt and we hate disorder.

PATRIOTS HATE DISORDER: CLOSE THE BORDER!

Nazi guilt has led to flooding the refined west with illegals fed by the charities of churches no less.

Anyone wanting to erase the borders of my beautiful country is my foe-- the disgusting enemy.

The worst and dumbest rise to the highest places in the land. That happens in evil eras, man.

Those who scream "racism" are the biggest racists and that's basic about these divisive fascists.

The liberal psycho gun-haters are wrong. If armed they won't be killed like the doomed throng.

The elite invent grievances before they exist. Then it's created and that's the crooked gov twist.

Blacks are hurt most with this mass immigration but aren't protesting in fear of execution.

2 parents provide structure = good kids. Government rewards parentless families = prison camps.

The Middle East was so different before this--classy, artistic, refined, Western dressed.

We allowed the culture to destroy our families through secular humanism and atheism, amen?

The prayer of one good man changes a nation--that's what the bible says, so get prayin.

LIBERAL CHAOS & ROT

Our speech will be banned in six months. We can't even say "he" or "she" as we sink to the depths.

Liberalism used to mean free thought and debate. Not anymore--you hold to the party line, a bore.

PC IS MIND CONTROL TO CREATE DIVISION

Political correctness is mind control meant to create division, hamstring debate and kill renaissance.

They think they're smart due to "elite" schools but due to liberalism they're dumb/not truly cool.

100 million killed last century by socialists and you dumb liberals wanted Bernie Sanders--idiots.

They're not truly dumb just brainwashed not to want freedom--they label that as slavery, in sum.

How silly can this get? But silliness doesn't make it any less dangerous as they close in the net.

Free societies do not have "state ideologies" but gov punishes thought without apologies.

Democrat Debates: not a word about ISIS, Euro-migrant crises or nuke deal-- inconceivable.

Officials mystified as to why locals have a problem with mass migration into their tiny towns (IQ down).

The UN seeks to criminalize "climate change denial". We have to accept this stuff that's in style.

Even if low-info voters did know about what's happening, they still don't care or are napping.

When you have no say on how your lives are run, life sux--no fun. The more   local   the   more   you.

LIBERAL CHAOS & ROT

With violence cops will be so busy in the cities maybe they'll leave us alone: the rural preppies.

We don't let our people have ideas so why would we let them have guns? Stalin

Beautiful music and mosques is about religion which diverts you from the Savior: God and Person.

State's Rights is the way to save our nation overnight. Not the feds or UN-- they're a blight.

Yes we could be killed any moment by an (all-departnemt's) SWAT team busting in like hoods.

100 MILLION KILLED AND THEY WANT SANDERS/CORTEZ?

100 million killed for socialism and you wanted socialist Sanders, how can I respect this?

It used to be armies conquered countries now it's banking combines and giant immigrant floods of the unrefined.

Trump's brashness is unprecedented in modern politics as the old leftist regime dies in public.

The culmination of 50 years of hippies is seen in the horrific heartless deceptions of Hillary.

44 years after Roe vs. Wade: how dark, dirty, debauched and dumbed down we became.

Cops concerned protecting Trump people would further inflame socialist mob. Lame excuse, hah.

The bathroom rule is a damnable heresy, saying it's the "golden rule"-- he'll self-destruct soon.

Mock the name of Jesus, destroy morality in a nation. All those who forget God will reap a whirlwind.

LIBERAL CHAOS & ROT

Bad leaders bash the bible because: It speaks against tyrants (like the black uniformed fuzz).

Are you kiddin? Despite what docs say a deadly poison is not a life-saving medicine.

A half a century since Roe vs. Wade and what do we see? Thugs, nags, evil kings and the dregs.

FRUGI-FATARIAN-FASTARIANISM

People usually don't die from starvation, they die from malnutrition from eating crap all day man.

Simple as pie, no hunger: Smoothie in morning, guacamole and salad brunch. Fast for dinner/wake up winner.

Cows walk by my house twice a week and I feed em apples. You think I could eat steak too? Impossible.

HOLY FAUCET, ENDLESS SPRING

It's an endless spring, a holy faucet. It's not me but it wells up in me then pops out like a bullet then I modify it.

No one can help me but the divine link chosen before my birth upon completion. That's how I think hon'.

What I feel for you is great/deep/intense but we don't get everything we want in life said the muse.

I'll wait on God/prepare for His perfect timing when I cross the great divide between the past and destiny.

3 psych depts: clinical, research and theoretical. One rare theoretician changes the paradigm every 40 years.

100 KAREN KELLOCK BOOKS

AFFINITY OR MISERY
AGELESS CORNUCOPIA
AMERICA AWAKE!
AMERICA'S DAFT ERA
ARTS OF PALEO FASTING
AUTOPHAGY ON CHEATERS
BACKSTABBING NEUROTICS
BETRAYAL TRAUMA
BOOMERS AND BROKENNESS
BOOT ON NECK
CHAMPION GUIDES
COMMIE NUTHOUSE
COMMIES
COMMUNIST SPIRIT
CONTAGION OF MADNESS
CONTAGIOUS MADNESS
CULTURE CLASH BASHED
DAFT LEFT
DAILY FASTARIAN
DAM RATS
DIVERSITY IS CRUELTY
E-RACE WHITE
EVIL FREAKS (Beyond Gross)
THE END OR A BEND?
FEMALE BULLIES AND FEMI-NAZIS
FEMALE CARNALITY
FEMALE DUMB DOWN
FEMALE POWER DRIVE
FEMINISM AND RUIN 1 & 2
FIX FOR MISFITS
FOOLS & TRAMPS
FREEDOM SPEAKING
FRENEMY ENABLER
FRENEMY LIAR
FRENEMY THIEF
FRENEMY TRAITOR
TRENEMY TYRANT
GENIUS IS HELD DOWN
GLOBALISLAM
GOD USES THE FLAWED
HAZE OF THE LATTER DAYS

AUTHOR BIO

Karen Kellock Ph.D.

Ph.D Political Psychology, UCI 1976
Post-Doctoral: UCI Medical School
Department of Psychiatry
Grants NIMH, NIAAA

Ph.D. dissertation "A Systems-Theoretic View of Pathologic Interaction" made an early mark as the "Wife of the Alcoholic Syndrome". Postdoctoral research at UCI Medical, Dept. of Psychiatry on the systems surrounding pathology on NIMH and NIAAA federal grants: The Contagion of Madness: The Psychology of Neurotic Interaction and Pathological Systems. Therapy tool Therapeutic Playwriting introduced the play Mary and Murv: Gruesome Twosomes in the Alcoholic Marriage. She taught Abnormal Psychology and Pathological Systems Theory at UC and CSU campuses and developed "the Debris Theory of Disease" in 100 books and website: (www.karenkellock.org).